ADVISOR AT RISK

ADVISOR AT RISK

A ROADMAP TO PROTECTING YOUR BUSINESS

ELLEN BESSNER

BABIN
BESSNER
SPRY

Dedicated to

Danielle and Nathan

TABLE OF CONTENTS

ACKNOWLEDGMENTS

Throughout my career, I have received overwhelming support from many people. My clients—the people working for institutions, big and small—have given me the opportunity to grow my practice and learn how this industry operates, from the inside out. Through my presentations, these institutions and many industry organizations have given me access to thousands of advisors who encouraged me to write this book.

When I decided to write *Advisor at Risk*, I contacted several Canadian business writers, each of whom gave me excellent advice. There are too many writers to mention, but I would be remiss not to acknowledge Carol Hansell, who wrote *Corporate Governance, What Directors Need to Know*. I was inspired by the author's elegance, charm, and intelligence, all of which are reflected in her book. Dan Richards, a well-known author (*Getting Clients, Keeping Clients*) and speaker in this industry, was a great marketing advisor. Thanks to journalist Ellin Bessner, who helped to promote this book and is a great cousin and friend.

Several compliance, sales, and regulatory folk, including Lorne Switzer, Dave Velanoff, and Maureen Jensen, have provided me with ongoing support. Ken Rosenberg has been a great mentor.

With respect to the content of this book, I can thank no one more than my friend and law firm partner Steven Sofer, who read several very early drafts and gave me big picture ideas that led to major improvements. Caroline Cakebread, introduced to me by Marlene Puffer, helped me immensely when she offered to read and advise me on the reorganization of a very early draft—this, before she had even met me.

My publisher, Penny Shore, introduced to me by Lana Marks Pulver and Kerri Marks Chetner, has been instrumental in her guidance, advice, and support in bringing this book to market. That includes introducing me to invaluable editors Dianne Maley and Karen Hoffmann-Zak, and to designer Eddie Chan all of whom brought this book to life; and to Paul Ornstein, who helped me to maintain the quality of the book. A special thanks to photographer David Batten, who had the challenge of taking a picture of me that my family didn't hate.

Five readers gave me insightful feedback on the final drafting of this work: my good friend Carol Church, introduced to me by Bindu Dhaliwal; Stephanie McManus, Robert Klosa, Chris Kruczynski, and Dirk Hohmann.

The drive and determination to write this book comes from the strength and encouragement of family members Evelyn Bessner, Jeff Bessner, Merle Bessner, and Ronda Bessner; and from close friends Constance Marlatt and Darina Harsaghy.

Words, written or verbal, are insufficient to express my gratitude to my children Nathan Bessner and Danielle Bessner for their immeasurable and continuous support, patience, and encouragement.

Ellen

INTRODUCTION

This book is for investment advisors, financial advisors, insurance agents and brokers, their supervisors, colleagues, assistants, and the companies they represent in the financial, investment, and insurance industries. Readers of this book may include registered representatives working for broker/dealers; financial advisors; branch managers; portfolio managers; financial planners; certified financial analysts; mutual fund salespeople; dually-licensed individuals who also work as insurance agents in a captive sales force; independent brokers; or any one of the many people who work in the offices of these licensed professionals.

The message is that investment and insurance products have become more complex, regulators more watchful, and clients more willing to sue. In short, the advisor's world has become more dangerous. Some say it's a matter of when, not if, an advisor will be hauled in front of a regulator or judge by an angry client. When that happens, how prepared are advisors to defend themselves?

As defense counsel, I hear heartbreaking stories from people in the financial and insurance services industry. They talk about what happens to them when clients complain or—worse—sue. It's not pretty. I disguise these stories, so that no one is identified and relay them in seminars I provide to advisors across North America. I tell these stories to help advisors appreciate the risks and build a roadmap toward managing that risk. Seminar attendees fear being the next one subject to a complaint. Nevertheless, they soak in my attempt at humor and my true passion for this industry. My goal is that they gain a new outlook, new strategies, and a renewed commitment toward building a compliant business. The problem is I am not very funny and, in any event, my seminars have a limited reach. That's why I wrote this book. I want to equip many more people—advisors, supervisors and the companies and people they work with across North America—with the tools necessary to reduce their risk. As professionals, advisors need to be alert to potential problems before they explode into client complaints that lead to regulatory investigations or litigation. I hope that advisors who read this book will gain a new perspective on their roles and responsibilities and will learn how to minimize their risks. Although the book is for all industry participants, the last part of each chapter contains a checklist of actions written specifically for advisors.

This book is not a legal text. For ease of reading, the legal principles most often relevant to advisors and branch managers have been described in broad, general strokes. In regard to specific issues of concern, advisors and branch managers will need to seek legal advice. I do, however, present and analyze many examples in the hope that readers will learn from the mistakes of others. The examples cited recount common problems faced by advisors and dealers in the financial services industry. I hope you will find this book useful.

EB

CHAPTER 1
Roles and Responsibilities

"Can't you make this go away?" my client pleads.
"Will I lose my license?" he asks. "Will I lose my job?"
"Can this really go on for years?" another client asks.
"It's the first thing I think of when I wake up in the morning,
  if I can sleep at all."
"What will they say in my community?"
They are advisors whose clients are suing them or who are defending themselves against a regulatory complaint. As defense counsel for dealers, advisors, and agents in the financial industry, I hear these worries expressed regularly.

Why do clients sue? Usually because they lost money and they're looking to the advisor, dealer, or insurance company to recover it, as is their legal right. Yet, many advisors faced with such complaints reflect on their meetings with the complaining clients and recall that the clients were sufficiently knowledgeable and, therefore, able to understand the products. The advisor remembers that the explanation of the product risks seemed clear to the client. Red flags were not apparent to the advisor at the beginning of the relationship. But later, when the market turns and the client complains, the client's memory paints a picture completely different than what the advisor remembers. At this juncture, advisors have everything to lose because their integrity, reputation, and license are on the line. It is ultimately the advisor's word against the client's, and without a paper trail, advisors and dealers are vulnerable.

The cost goes well beyond the financial. Distracted by the stress of unresolved complaints—no matter how groundless they may seem—advisors say that they cannot concentrate on their work, lose confidence in their abilities, and begin to question themselves. This stress directly and significantly affects every aspect of their lives. Many confess their personal relationships suffer from the stress they experience over the months and sometimes years—yes years—that it takes to conclude the matter.

With the wisdom of hindsight, advisors who face these problems wish they could turn back the clock so that they could do things differently. While that is impossible, my hope is that readers can learn from the experience of other advisors who, unfortunately, were not equipped with the proper tools and training to render their businesses compliant with all the relevant rules and regulations.

I don't believe that compliance can be shoved down someone's throat. It needs to be explained so that advisors, supervisors, and senior executives understand the benefits, are motivated to follow the rules, and appreciate the risks of not doing so. Let's start with the basics:

- What are the demands on advisors and dealers?
- What are advisors' roles, goals, and duties?
- What are the risks that advisors and dealers face that threaten their livelihood?

I. DEMANDS

CLIENTS' DEMANDS

Too often, clients refuse to spend enough time with their advisors or to disclose their personal information, which advisors are legally required to obtain before opening accounts. As well, clients will often not trouble themselves to understand explanations provided by advisors and dealers, or to read the material they are given. Certain clients have unreasonable expectations of returns on investments, expecting every investment to yield positive returns that exceed the market benchmarks all the time. Client expectations and demands can far exceed what advisors and dealers can consistently deliver.

REGULATORY DEMANDS

Regulators are becoming more demanding and threatening, imposing larger penalties and longer suspensions. Dealers are charged with the responsibility of ensuring that every member of their organization, particularly licensed staff, meets and exceeds regulatory requirements. Dealers are scrutinized by accountants hired by regulators to perform periodic audits and by retired police officers hired to perform investigations. Directors and officers are at risk personally for regulatory infractions.

PRODUCT DEMANDS

Products are becoming more complex and numerous and are forever changing. The risk factors are increasingly difficult to understand and explain to clients. Advisors are required to understand each product and the associated risks in much more detail than is provided in marketing presentations, so that these can be explained to the client.

COURTS

Judges order payment of damages for losses on investments even when clients are sophisticated and experienced investors. Judges have made it clear that they hold advisors to standards that far exceed anything previously understood by advisors, supervisors, and dealers. Why? Because advisors have licenses, codes of conduct, and internal policies and procedures—and investors don't!

EDUCATION

While qualifying courses permit professionals to be licensed, most admit that they learn less in school and more on the job. However, on the job, the focus may seem to be more on building an advisor's book of business and less on managing compliance risk. Advisors know the simple equation that revenue minus expenses equals profitability, but their focus must turn to the expense side of the equation. Their education must emphasize how compliance risk can lead to increased expenses. Advisors need to appreciate that if they don't take the time and spend the resources to gain a better understanding of their regulatory and legal risks and obligations, their profitability will suffer.

Understanding the rules and ensuring that they are complied with cannot be a second priority. While regulators and independent organizations prepare materials to teach investing clients about the steps to take to sue their advisors, only a few courses exist that support advisors with compliance training and help them identify risks and protect themselves.

COMPLIANCE DEPARTMENT DEMANDS

The compliance department has been perceived as an expense that interferes with advisors building their book. However, the reality is that advisors who do not value compliance will not survive in this industry. Dealers that do not have, or do not follow, compliance procedures will be at the mercy of their clients, regulators, and judges.[1]

If advisors learn to better appreciate their roles and risks, more complaints and lawsuits can be avoided and, indeed, more clients will be satisfied.

II. ROLES, GOALS, AND DUTIES

Advisors are experts in a complex and continually changing industry that offers an expanding list of investment and insurance products. They are held to the same standards as other professionals, including doctors and lawyers. The following quotation, from a frequently cited case, makes this clear:

". . . financial advisors must be taken to assume duties similar to those of any other professional advisor—doctor, accountant, engineer, lawyer. . . to ensure that customers or clients are aware of available options, and of the main potential benefits and risks associated with them."[2]

A doctor provides medical advice, a lawyer provides legal advice, and advisors in the financial and insurance industry provide investment or insurance advice. A common misconception in this industry is that advisors are salespeople only, selling insurance and investment products rather than professional advisory services. However, advisors must change the way they think about their roles. They are not salespeople but professionals, providing a balanced approach in the best interests of the client.

---

1.   The role of compliance will be discussed in greater detail in Chapter 10.
2.   *Rhoads v. Prudential – Bache Securities Canada Ltd.* (1992), 63 B.C.L.R. (2d) 256 at p.262

Advisors are obliged to operate with the utmost integrity and to always put their clients' interests first when choosing a product or strategy. In other words, advisors cannot factor their own personal benefit into advice they give clients.

Knowing each of one's clients is the cornerstone of this industry because one cannot ascertain which investment or insurance products suit clients without knowing their specific objectives and risk tolerance.

III. RISKS

Advisors have to withstand the scrutiny of those judging them: regulators, trial judges, the press, and the investing public. Advisors have been the target of client complaints, regulatory investigations, litigation proceedings, and damaging press releases. The effect of a single client complaint can be devastating. Advisors must learn how to recognize and anticipate problems before they occur and incorporate the tools described in this book to ward them off.

WHAT ARE THE MAIN RISKS?

Markets Rise and Fall

Market participants are happy in a bull market. Advisors and clients alike are lulled into a false sense of security when the value of their holdings increases. But we all know that markets rise and fall. Unfortunately, even the most successful advisors, analysts, and industry gurus cannot accurately and consistently predict just when these movements might happen. Advisors need to remind their clients that they do not have a crystal ball.

When the market fails to recover promptly and clients realize that their losses could be permanent, greed can sometimes turn to fear, and some clients may turn to the obvious scapegoats—advisors and dealers, the perceived deep pockets.

Risk Tolerance in a Bull Market

In a bull market, clients can present themselves as risk tolerant when they are really only excited about the potential improvement in their portfolios. The bull market often creates an unreasonable increase in client expectations, as opposed to a greater appetite for risk. When prices are rising, clients have been known to refuse to allow their advisors to rebalance their portfolios by selling a portion of their fastest-growing and higher-risk investments. They may even want to buy more. When markets are strong or a particular investment or sector is hot, clients, spurred on by the media, may push advisors to purchase unsuitable investments or to over-concentrate their accounts in one sector. However, when prices fall, those same clients do not hesitate to blow the whistle or complain to regulators that their investments were inappropriate and improperly diversified. Advisors are at risk if they don't recognize that a bull market can sometimes disguise a client's true risk tolerance.

In these circumstances, judges and arbitrators have ruled in favor of the client, if the investments were indeed unsuitable or over-concentrated in one product or sector. The advisor may be ordered to reimburse the client for losses, even though the client wanted the investments in the first place.

Failure to Manage Clients' Expectations

To avoid the mood swings that come with soaring and dipping markets, advisors must manage their clients' expectations of investment returns over the long term. The market may be up 35% so far in a given year, but the average annual gain is much less than that over several years. The implication is clear: in some years prices fall. If the average annual return for a given investment class is 7% over the past 30 years, and an advisor's clients are pressing him to make 15%, they are expecting a level of performance that their advisor may not be able to deliver consistently. Failure to manage clients' expectations can lead to substantial risks in the form of litigation and regulatory complaints.

Communication Risk

Most communication between advisors and clients is oral. The risk with oral communication is that it can be misinterpreted, taken out of context, or forgotten. When advisors are optimistic about a particular investment or insurance product, they tend not to focus on the disadvantages, costs, or possible risks. Similarly, some clients tend to focus only on a product's advantages and only hear what they want to hear, disregarding the advisor's warnings about possible risks.

Client complaints commonly arise from lack of communication or a breakdown in communication, particularly in a falling market. It is common for clients to say that they understood mere projections to be guarantees or, at time of purchase, to tell the advisor they understand, but later on deny having understood.

Credibility Risk

The issue of witness credibility plays a significant role in judges' decisions. In court or at a regulatory hearing, the client and advisor each tell their version of the events to a judge or arbitrator. The same events are often described by the client and the advisor in diametrically opposed terms. It may be that they both attempt to describe the events as best they can but, no doubt, people's biases affect their recollection of what happened.

Consider this scenario:

Client:

"I was referred to Mac (the advisor) many years ago. I was invited to one of his free seminars in which he described the type of investing he was doing for his clients. I knew nothing about investing, but Mac explained that I could make much more money than what I was making on GICs (Guaranteed Investment Certificates). I worked hard all my life, and Mac said this was an opportunity to get my money to work for me. I liked the concept, but I didn't understand that there was risk involved. Mac never talked to me about the risks of investing. I totally trusted him and followed his advice because he promised that I would make more money following his advice than if I left my money where it was. When I received my statements, I didn't understand them, but Mac reassured me that this was the way to go, and I should just follow his advice. I can't believe how much money I lost. I am now 62-years-old and I need to continue to work to make back the money I lost. I am mad at Mac, and I have found a lawyer to help me get my money back by suing Mac and his employer."

The advisor's version of events is different:

"Mr. Kirk (the client) was a friend of my father. I had been helping my father with his investments for years, and Mr. Kirk, who was invested in GICs, watched my father's retirement savings improve. My father took trips and bought new cars while Mr. Kirk lived more carefully. Mr. Kirk was getting restless and wanted to switch to mutual funds. I explained to him that while I would put him in mutual funds and conservative stocks, there would be no guarantees, like there are with GICs, and there was risk of loss of capital. I invited him to one of my seminars in which I explained the potential growth of mutual funds and, specifically, historical evidence that they yield better returns than GICs over the long term.

Mr. Kirk approached me after the seminar, wanting to meet with me immediately. We agreed to meet the next day. I was pleased that Mr. Kirk wanted to invest with me, but I was a bit worried because my father told me that he is a big complainer. I wanted to help Mr. Kirk, so I agreed to take his account. Well, about nine months later, the market fell, and Mr. Kirk called me when he received his statement. I told him not to worry; he was still three years from retirement, and these were investments for the long term. Mr. Kirk couldn't handle it, even though I had previously explained the risks to him. He instructed me to liquidate his portfolio and send him a check. He issued a complaint to the regulator and sued me for his losses."

It becomes the client's word against the advisor's and, as with other professionals, the onus is on advisors to prove that they fulfilled their duties to a reasonable standard. This is very difficult to prove without documentary evidence reflecting the discussions with the client. When it is client versus advisor, courts tend to sympathize with the client.

Clients are Viewed with Sympathy

Advisors—and this applies to other professionals such as doctors, lawyers, and accountants—are assumed to be better educated, more knowledgeable, and more experienced in their respective fields than their clients. Indeed, clients seek out, rely upon, and pay for professional advice. Accordingly, clients are perceived as vulnerable and reliant upon the better-educated, knowledgeable, and experienced advisors. That's why courts and regulators tend to view clients sympathetically. It's also why advisors have to bolster their cases with documentary evidence.

Risk of Losing One's Most Valuable Assets: Reputation, License, and Money

Advisors' most valuable assets are their reputation, license, and money. A single regulatory investigation, client complaint, or lawsuit threatens all three assets—for both the advisor and the dealer. Clients may turn on their advisors because of a loss. This may result in a complaint to the regulator or the dealer and, ultimately, to legal proceedings.

Reputation

Once the local newspaper becomes interested in the subject, the publicity can wreak havoc on the reputation of the dealer and the advisor. In fact, with the Internet and e-mail, the publicity can travel far beyond the jurisdiction in which the action is commenced or the complaint filed.

It is easy for a reporter to get a copy of the claim, because it is a public document, filed in the local court offices, and can be obtained for a nominal photocopying fee. All legal documents that follow the filing of the claim, including the defense and any sworn affidavits and court orders, are available to the public. Newspaper reporters can monitor the litigation and continue to report on the allegations, even if they are unfounded, unsubstantiated, and unproven. These publications avoid a claim for defamation merely by stating that the allegations have not been proven in court.

Even if the judge does not find the advisor or dealer responsible for payment and dismisses the plaintiff's claim, newspaper articles reporting the allegations have already damaged the advisor's and dealer's reputations. Wouldn't it be grand if the advisor's and dealer's exoneration were given equal press coverage?

One client complaint can shatter a lifetime of hard work, not to mention one's confidence. Advisors rely on referrals from existing clients to expand their business. Advisors who have tarnished reputations will be unable to expand from their existing client base, because comments made to potential clients will not result in favorable recommendations. Further, referrals can operate in reverse, as clients share negative endorsements and one complaint turns into an avalanche of complaints.

How can advisors protect their reputations, their most valuable asset? The simple answer is by incorporating the techniques that are described in this book.[3] However, one must first understand and learn to identify the risks.

License

A license is not a right but a privilege. It is granted only to those who fulfill specified requirements. The regulators are the watchdogs. They grant the license and have authority to revoke or suspend it.[4]

Without a license, advisors cannot advise on the purchase or sale of securities or insurance products. Accordingly, if advisors lose their license, they lose their main source of revenue. A license is a valuable asset.

Money

Like most professionals, an advisor's goal is to build his or her business through a reputation for honesty and hard work. In growing their businesses, many advisors rely on referrals from satisfied clients. As advisors' assets under administration grow, so, too, do their commissions and/or fees.

However, a single regulatory investigation or lawsuit can be extremely costly and can turn an advisor's success into immediate failure. In addition to legal costs, significant penalties may be

---

3. To be cautious, however, and to ensure the changes are made in a manner that is most efficient, and most consistent with the dealer's internal policies, advisors may want to check with their branch manager or compliance officer before implementing the changes suggested in this book.
4. Judges in court do not have such authority.

imposed by the regulator and by a judge awarding damages. There are also hidden costs including opportunity costs that result from time advisors spend with lawyers or with the regulator, and/or being distracted by the stress of the outstanding matter, instead of working to build their business and earn more money.

Dealer Risk

Advisors in most North American jurisdictions are not permitted to sell securities without being registered with a regulator, through a dealer. If they sell insurance, they must be employed by an insurance company or associated with an MGA (Managing General Agent) or AGA (Associate General Agent). Advisors under investigation or subject to a client complaint, worry that the investigation or complaint may jeopardize their relationship with their dealer/employer/MGA/AGA. Regardless of whether it is an employment relationship or an independent contractual one, a serious infraction may lead to termination.[5] Advisors embroiled in these matters may have difficulty finding another dealer, insurance company, MGA, or AGA through which they can operate their businesses, and may be denied errors and omissions insurance. This can end an otherwise lucrative career.

The Risk of Focusing Exclusively on Revenue

Advisors who exclusively focus on growing their business and ignore danger signs, accepting every client regardless of risk and neglecting to manage or decline clients with unrealistic expectations, are heading for big problems.[6] The balance of this book will identify the red flags and will provide a roadmap to growing revenue without compromising advisors and their reputations.

---

5.   Dealers can impose penalties and can require the advisor to be more closely supervised through internal controls.
6.   These topics will be explored and discussed in detail in Chapters 7 and 8.

SUMMARY

Regulatory complaints or litigation carry significant costs, both financial and personal. It is crucial for advisors to clearly understand their roles and responsibilities, so that they can ensure that they fulfill the required demands and avoid or minimize the risks.

ADVISORS TAKE ACTION

✓ Understand the demands of your industry and meet your obligations as a professional.

✓ Understand the product and its risks and communicate these to the client. The risks include rising and falling markets and an advisor's inability to predict the market.

✓ Identify whether clients have indeed increased their risk tolerance, particularly in a bull market, and don't just take their word for it. Don't let clients push you to purchase unsuitable investments or to over-concentrate their accounts in one security or sector.

✓ Remember, judges are sympathetic to clients. To ensure your version of events is preferred by the judge or arbitrator, ensure that you have documentation to prove it.

✓ Manage your clients' expectations to protect your reputation, license, and money.

✓ Don't focus exclusively on revenue but consider the expense side of your business, which in part reflects your compliance. This will have a direct effect on profitability.

CHAPTER 2
Professionalism

Many advisors in the financial industry tend to focus more on selling products than on giving professional advice. They may think of themselves exclusively as salespeople. Although most advisors are remunerated with commissions, they should not confuse their roles with that of salespeople. Selling products is only one part of the service they offer.

I contrast the role of a professional advisor with that of a salesperson selling a suit. The salesperson does not need a license to sell a suit. In determining the needs of a shopper, he has neither a regulatory nor a legal obligation to "know his customer." Take me for example. Do I need the suit for work? Do I travel and need the suit not to crease when squished inside a small suitcase? Am I a slob who needs dark colors or patterns that hide remnants of my lunch, helping me to avoid embarrassment at meetings? The salesperson can sell me a white linen suit, far beyond what my pocketbook can bear. I am unaware of any regulatory obligation the salesperson has to ensure that the purchase is appropriate and will meet my personal needs.

Professionals are different. They must determine their clients' needs and advise them accordingly. To succeed in this industry, advisors need to understand what that means. Professionalism is fundamental to the success or failure of advisors and dealers because they are held to the very same standards as other professionals, including doctors, lawyers, accountants, and architects.[1]

This standard was established in a case in which a retired couple lost 22% of their nest egg.[2] Mr. and Mrs. Rhoads were a couple who sold

---

1. *Rhoads v. Prudential–Bache Securities Canada Ltd.* [1992] 2 I.E. 630 (B.C.C.A.); 63 B.C.L.R. (2d) 256.
2. Rhoads, *Ibid.* at 258.

their business in California in the '80s and moved to western Canada to retire. They did so when the US dollar was significantly stronger than the Canadian dollar. They placed the proceeds from the sale of their business into Guaranteed Investment Certificates, which were earning 10% per annum at the time.

They responded to a newspaper advertisement and attended an advisor's free presentation, after which they retained the advisor and directed him to invest their money to earn more than the yield on their GICs and yet ensure the capital was 100% protected. Disregarding the clients' instructions and risk tolerance, the advisor placed the money in three growth-oriented mutual funds and in the retractable preference shares of two different companies.

In the fall of 1987, just before the big market meltdown, Mr. and Mrs. Rhoads left on a cruise, providing the advisor with the name of the cruise ship and their daughter's contact information. They returned from their cruise to learn that they had lost 22% of their capital. Concerned that they would lose more, they decided to liquidate their investments on October 29, 1987, thereby crystallizing their losses.

The judge ruled in favor of Mr. and Mrs. Rhoads, finding the investments unsuitable in light of their instructions to preserve the capital 100%. The dealer and advisor were ordered to compensate them and pay damages in the amount of $132,787.81, plus costs and interest. The judge concluded that the advisor's inability to prove that he informed the couple of the risks of the investment meant that he did not fulfill his professional obligations.

How can we incorporate professionalism into advisors' everyday practices, so that they can meet or surpass the required standard? Communication is central to the professional advisor's duty.

I.   COMMUNICATION: MANAGE CLIENT EXPECTATIONS

Managing clients' expectations is an important way for advisors to protect themselves from client complaints. I always say under-promise, over-perform. For example, I ask clients for a deadline when they ask me to deliver a piece of work, regardless of what it is. If they say they need it in a week, whether it is an opinion, a pleading, or a letter, I try to deliver it within five days. If they ask me when I will be in a position to deliver the document, I suggest 10 days, knowing that it is likely I can deliver it in seven. Always exceed expectations when you are in the service industry, and your clients will have less reason to complain or sue you.

Managing expectations should begin before the advisor accepts the person as a client. Both the client and the advisor should interview each other to ensure a good match. It is not just the client who is interviewing the advisor. The advisor should interview the client to determine whether this is a person with whom he or she can work. It is important to establish two things: 1) that an advisor's way of working and areas of expertise can properly help the potential client, and 2) the client's expectations—making sure these expectations match what the advisor can actually do for the client to ensure that the relationship is a good fit for both parties. These things are important to determine at the beginning of the relationship, because it is much more difficult to manage a client's expectations once a relationship has already been firmly established.

To manage clients' expectations, advisors must appreciate the importance of careful listening and the effect that their advice has on clients. The next portion of this chapter will examine listening and speaking, two seemingly simple concepts that can significantly impact an advisor's success or failure. Then we will examine different tools that a professional advisor can employ to successfully listen and speak.

LISTENING

Why is listening important?

Part of the process of transforming from a salesperson into a professional advisor is learning to appreciate the value of listening. Salespeople tend to believe that if they continue to talk, the customer will buy what they are selling.

When I began to market training programs to banks, dealers, and insurance companies, I made hundreds of cold calls. Even though my credentials, being a partner in a large and reputable law firm, made it easy for me to get most senior compliance people to talk to me, I found that I could not "close the deal." I turned to various books on selling, including one of my favorites, *Mastering the Complex Sale*, and realized I was making a fundamental error; I was talking too much and not listening enough.[3] By listening, one can ascertain client needs and make suggestions that fit those needs. I decided to change my tack. Instead of talking, I listened.

Of course, to get the client to talk, the advisor needs to ask the appropriate questions to elicit relevant information.

Open-Ended Questions

Open-ended questions, such as questions that begin with "why," "how," and "what," invite clients to explain fully and elicit answers more detailed than "yes" or "no." For example: "What will it be important for you to do during your retirement?" This is a question that will elicit discussion. Contrast that question with, "Do you intend to travel after you retire?" The client may have some retirement plans, but he may not think his advisor needs this information if she only asks a narrow question that invites a "yes" or "no" answer.

While listening carefully to the client's answers describing his or her expectations, the advisor should not interrupt. Instead, the advisor should listen, take notes, and attempt to ascertain whether the client's expectations can be achieved. Listening carefully to the answers is crucial if the advisor wants to identify potential problems. Below are a few examples of some open-ended questions an advisor might ask at the first client meeting. The advisor may want to be more subtle than what is suggested to avoid offending the client:

What is your experience with past advisors?
Red light answer: "I hated her!"
Green light answer: "I like him but I just moved, so I need someone a little closer to where I live."

How many advisors have you worked with in the past?
Red light answer: "I have had...let's see...6 or 7 advisors, I think one was worse than the next."
Green light answer: "Only one."

---

3.   Thull, Jeff. *Mastering the Complex Sale*. New Jersey: John Wiley & Sons, Inc., 2003.

Why are you looking for a new advisor?

Red light answer: "It's none of your business."

Green light answer: "He manages my wife's accounts, and she and I agreed that I would move my money to another broker in light of our recent separation and impending divorce."

What are the things you liked best about your last advisor?

Red light answer: "Well, she was great looking; she had a nice office; and…um…I can't think of anything else—she was a dolt—but good looking. Did I tell you what she looked like?"

Green light answer: "She was responsive—she answered all my questions directly and always called me back the same day that I left her a message. She didn't speak over my head."

What are three things you didn't like about your last advisor?

Red light answer: "Okay, one, he lost me money. Two, he never gave me good advice. Three, I could do a better job myself. Four, oh—did you say three?—because I can think of more, like he was always asking me personal questions about my other assets. I think he had nerve."

Green light answer: "That's a hard question to answer. He was really terrific. If we hadn't moved away to another town, I would have continued working with him."

How did you get along with your advisor?

Red light answer: "He was nice at first but, when I started losing money, well, we started to fight."

Follow-up question: What did you disagree about and how was it resolved?

Red light answer: "I sued the ----! He ended up admitting he was wrong and paying me back what I had lost."

Green light answer: "No problem at all—we got along fine."

What are your expectations concerning reporting? Do you like your advisor to call, or send e-mails or letters to keep in touch and ensure the account operates to your satisfaction?

Red light answer: "I don't want to hear from you—just make me money!"

Green light answer: "E-mail is great, but I want to be sure I can call you with questions and meet with you once or twice a year."

Are you interviewing other advisors before you determine who you will be working with?

Red light answer: "Yes, I want the best returns for the least amount of commissions. So, I am shopping around."

Green light answer: "No—why would I do that?" Or, "I am interviewing three advisors to get the right fit."

How have you chosen your advisors in the past?

Red light answer: "I don't know; there have been so many."

Green light answer: "Personality and expertise are important to me."

What do you know about our dealer?

Red light answer: "It is big so if I lose money, I have a deep pocket to sue."

Green light answer: "I have some comfort because it is a reputable organization."

What is your knowledge level and, by that, I mean, what do you know about different types of investment products, and what is your experience?

Red light answer: "I don't need to know anything—that's why I have an advisor."

Green light answer: "Not a lot but I have a basic understanding."

How do you feel about sharing personal financial information with your advisor?

Red light answer: "It's none of your business."

Green light answer: "As long as he keeps it private, that's fine."

If the advisor listens closely to what clients say in response to more subtle questions concerning their experience with advisors, she will gather the information required to determine whether she can meet a particular client's expectations, or whether she even wants to try. Advisors should be particularly wary of clients who have unreasonable expectations.

Clients who provide complete and thoughtful answers will guide advisors to follow-up questions, enabling them to better understand their client's expectations and to determine whether they can be managed appropriately. Those follow-up questions should be asked only after the client has completed her thought. So as not to forget a follow-up question or expression of concern, advisors should jot down a reminder note—do not interrupt! Once the client has completed her thought, the advisor can clarify mixed messages. For example, a client says she is not risk averse but cannot afford to lose any capital. After listening carefully, the advisor will want to be certain to ask her what exactly she means. It is the advisor's job to distinguish between the client's willingness to assume risk and her capacity to bear it.[4]

SPEAKING

How can advisors speak in a way that clients will understand? Advisors must speak the client's language in order to manage the client's expectations. In other words, advisors should leave acronyms and technical language out of their vocabulary. I use the analogy of a person speaking Hungarian while explaining the risks of an investment to a person who doesn't understand Hungarian. Speak the client's language.

Some advisors ask me what they should do if the client doesn't speak the same language they do and can't understand what they say.[5]

---

4. Note a problem on many risk tolerance questionnaires: they confirm that clients have an aggressive growth orientation even though clients, in answer to a question, indicated that they would sell their investments if the market dropped by 10%.
5. The advisor must be particularly cautious if the client does not understand disclosure documents or other documents the client needs to sign. Some firms have forms translated into different languages.

With the diversity of the North American population, this is common. I suggest that advisors refer clients who speak a different language to advisors who also speak that language. If that is not an option, then ensure that someone interprets who is not a beneficiary or a person with an interest in the client's estate. Often people who do not speak the same language as the advisor will bring their son or daughter to meetings to act as an interpreter. This can be dangerous and may present a conflict for the advisor, particularly when children of elderly clients misunderstand their roles. Instead of helping their parents to achieve what is in their best interest, grown children may behave as if they themselves are the clients. Advisors, too, may confuse the ultimate client—the parent—with the person assisting, especially if the son or daughter instructs the advisor to have the assets managed in a way that suits them and that is not in the best interests of the elderly parent.

Be careful when a relative or close friend of the client interprets. If the client sues the advisor, there will be two witnesses to support the client's version of events, and the lone advisor will have a more difficult time.

If the advisor does not know the client's language, he cannot be certain that his words have been accurately interpreted or that the instructions interpreted back to him are accurate. How can advisors be sure the client's expectations are managed if they don't know whether the client fully understands their explanations?

Equally as important as language is the message that is delivered and the tone used to deliver it.

NON-VERBAL COMMUNICATION

Advisors who exude professionalism in every aspect of their business will inspire clients to have more confidence in them as professionals. For example, the office should have privacy policies and ensure clients' information is kept private. When they are in the office, clients should not see the names of other clients on files or documents. Organized offices and client files reflect well on the advisor as a professional.[6]

---

6.   Privacy will be discussed in greater detail in Chapter 9.

II. TOOLS FOR THE PROFESSIONAL ADVISOR

Advisors can use several tools to meet their professional obligations. It is important for advisors to determine which tools work best and to customize them for each client.

I have found that both agendas and checklists are useful when prepared before each client meeting. Not only do these tools allow advisors to appear professional, they result in meetings that are much more focused and efficient. The ultimate result is financial success for the advisor.

Be careful not to rely solely on forms to the exclusion of other issues that may need to be raised. No single checklist or agenda fits every client. If advisors limit their discussions to items on a form, they may overlook other issues, thereby falling into the same pattern that I believe advisors have with the Know-Your-Client (KYC) Form or the insurance application. Advisors believe that all they need is the information listed on the form, and all they need to do is check off the boxes to fulfill their obligations. No single form, agenda, or checklist, however, contains all the client information that advisors need. The professional advisor must listen carefully to what each client says during the meeting to ensure that questions and issues pertinent to that particular client are asked, and relevant information is collected. The advisor is not a robot completing a form, but a professional who is truly interested in advising and assisting clients.

To ascertain which items to place on the agenda, first consider what needs to be achieved during the meeting. What is the purpose of the meeting? What might be important to discuss with the client at this stage in her life? Examine the notes from previous meetings to determine whether the client's goals were achieved.

A checklist or an agenda provides the advisor with a framework from which to build.

CHECKLIST

A checklist, like an agenda, is a useful tool to minimize one's note taking.[7] Instead of writing long sentences, one can tick off items

---

7.   Notes will be discussed more fully in Chapter 6.

on a checklist and scribble down other important information about what was discussed concerning the issues.

If there are new areas that an advisor wants to examine with a client such as explaining the risks outlined in the prospectus, these should be added to the checklist. Checklists need to be customized for each client meeting.

Checklists also serve as reminders to collect information or documents from the client, whether in the first meeting or later. A checklist can outline the list of items that the client agrees to deliver. This list and one's handwritten notes can be given to an assistant, who can summarize in a letter, the items the client agreed to deliver. The assistant can then follow up with the client to collect any missing items. Once all items are collected, the assistant can give the file to the advisor to complete.

Checklists are terrific for advisors licensed and/or registered to sell more than one type of product. For example, if the advisor is licensed to sell insurance and investment products, checklists can help to establish whether the client might be better served by a product other than the one requested. If the advisor's Web site lists five types of products for sale, ticking off a checklist will confirm that each item was offered to the client. It will also show which products were declined.[8]

Advisors may also want to develop a special checklist for clients who reach certain milestones, for example; getting married, having children, and approaching retirement. In fact, I suggest that advisors speak to clients about powers of attorney well before clients may need to rely on them.[9] An accident can happen, incapacitating a client at any age. Clients are never too young to be asked whether they have a will and/or power of attorney and the name of the agent, lawyer, or other person who has the original documents. These items can be added to the checklist.

---

8. Advisors who are dually licensed should not mix client checklists that contain a particular client's information on both insurance and securities. The client's insurance information should not end up in the dealer's file or vice versa. For privacy reasons, files on different subjects need to be segregated.
9. See more about powers of attorney in Chapter 8.

AGENDA

In contrast to a checklist, an agenda sets out topics and sub-topics that the advisor intends to discuss with a particular client. The agenda is prepared in advance of, and specifically for, the meeting.

A pre-printed agenda serves several purposes. If the advisor is organized in advance, having reviewed client files before any meetings or scheduled telephone calls with the client, then the agenda can be customized for the meeting to ensure all items are reviewed.

An agenda is not necessarily formal or rigid. I prepare an agenda before almost every meeting with a client. If I think of it far enough in advance, I might ask my assistant to format the agenda so that I can give a copy to the client at the beginning of the meeting. If I am very organized, I might send a copy to the client and ask whether she has any items to add. I have to admit, this is a rare event!

Advisors should use the agenda during the meeting to indicate which items were covered. This achieves two goals. First, it will form part of the evidence of topics that were discussed. Second, if plenty of space is left between items—or headings—it can help advisors organize their notes as the topics discussed can be expanded upon in writing, under the pre-printed headings.

III. ACTION

Regardless of what strategies are employed, it is important that everyone working in the advisor's office follow them consistently.

CONSISTENCY

Each member of the office is part of the team and should act professionally. Professionalism in every task is crucial to avoiding allegations of negligence. If each member complies and adheres to regulations, internal policies, and sound business practices, clients will be reminded of the group's professionalism.

Buy-in from staff is crucial. Staff should contribute to setting the rules, assuming that what is suggested complies with dealer policies and the laws and regulations of that jurisdiction. One more thing for advisors: if advisors set the rules, they should follow them. Over the years, I have interviewed assistants who complain that advisors set the office rules but are the first ones to bend or break them. For example, some offices use note-taking software, so that when clients call and someone in the office speaks to them, there is a record in the software system indicating who spoke to the client, the client's name, the date and time the client called, and a summary of the conversation. This way the next person who speaks to the client can ascertain from the electronic record what was discussed. Some of the assistants I spoke to indicated that they enter all pertinent information into the system, but the advisor does not consistently do so. Then, when the client calls, the assistant is uncertain of what was discussed. Either the client must be put to the trouble of having to repeat what was previously discussed or the assistant must insist that the client speak directly with the advisor. This is neither efficient for the advisor nor beneficial for the client.

ADHERENCE TO REGULATIONS / LAWS / INTERNAL POLICY

The failure by any team member to adhere to the compliance and internal rules set by the dealer is at the heart of many lawsuits. Evidence of non-compliance can bolster a client's case of negligence, against the advisor. If the client's lawyer detects a breach of regulation or dealer policy, this fact will be used to color the judge's view that the advisor was unprofessional—even if such a breach is unrelated to the allegations of negligence. For example, in some cases, investments are alleged to have been unsuitable, and a sloppy KYC form is used to bolster the client's case, even though the parts of the form that are proven wrong do not relate to the client's risk tolerance or financial objectives.

Policy manuals are sometimes ignored by team members. This is dangerous because as professionals in a highly regulated industry, advisors will be held to the standard of their internal policy manuals. It is also problematic that while policy manuals constantly change to reflect regulatory and system changes, the training of advisors and their team members is sometimes ignored. This is troublesome because the intent of training is to ensure that the entire team understands and follows the new policies and systems. Dealers, aware of this problem, hire me to review their internal policies. Then, I develop and present training to advisors to explain why the policies are important for managing their business risk. Some dealers rely on their internal compliance staff to do this training. It matters less who does the training than that it be done so compellingly that the advisor and the assistants appreciate the import of the new rules, policies, and systems. These new rules, policies, and systems need to be incorporated into the team's operations and must be routinely followed by all advisors and team members. The compliance trainer should not preach but should try to persuade the advisors, through role playing, guest speakers, or whatever works, that compliance is something they must do for themselves rather than for others. In the process, I have learned that humor goes further than bullying and is far more fun.

Keeping on top of rules and regulations in general is important. Breaches of regulation are also at the heart of the evidence against advisors in regulatory hearings and litigation. Because regulators issue numerous rules, bulletins, policies, and notices, it is difficult for advisors to remain on top of their obligations. As a result, the contents are neither understood nor accepted, and so the new rules are not put into practice until those who neglect or refuse to comply with changes face the threat of a penalty. Advisors who are told that they must make the transition to a new regulatory requirement, such as ensuring there are updated KYC forms for each client account, complain that their clients do not want to be bothered with new forms. However, if advisors understood that updating information allows them to become better acquainted with their clients to ensure investments are suitable, they might complete this task more willingly. Talking to clients more often could also boost business.

WHAT CAN AND CANNOT BE DELEGATED

Assistants or receptionists who greet clients at the office or on the telephone should understand their obligations to clients and the limits to their responsibilities, especially in regard to advising clients. Most assistants, licensed or not, are prohibited from giving clients advice. Nevertheless, assistants can be instrumental in helping the advisor build and maintain client relations by, among many other things, fielding calls and ensuring the advisor responds to client concerns expeditiously. The advisor should be careful never to ask assistants, licensed or not, to advise clients.[10]

In many regulatory complaints and litigation matters, clients allege that they found it impossible to contact their advisors. They say that they left several messages but never heard back from the advisor. When I question the complaining clients, I find that they contacted the assistants who dealt with the issues. The clients, however, continue to expect calls from their advisors. To avoid a breakdown in communication and dissatisfied clients, assistants should confirm at the end of each telephone conversation that the client is satisfied with the resolution of the issue and that there is no need for further action. A note in the file or indication in the electronic software system will resolve allegations that the advisor failed to or neglected to respond to telephone messages. A simple question from the assistant such as, "Have I dealt with all your concerns satisfactorily, or would you still like to hear from Joe (the advisor)?" will show that the issue has been resolved to the client's satisfaction. There is no need, then, for the advisor to phone the client.

In my office, I rely on my assistant to maintain a running list of obligations and deadlines. She follows up with me in advance of deadlines to ensure that I meet or exceed clients' expectations and my professional obligations. Very often she will say, "Did you hear from your client in regard to the draft response to the regulator's letter due in three days?" I may direct her to send an e-mail reminding the client that we need comments to meet the deadline set by the regulator. My assistant cannot, however, advise the client on the content of the letters. She can send me an e-mail with questions the client needs me to answer, or she can schedule a call with the client so that I can answer these questions. Some clients push assistants to answer questions they are not licensed to answer, promising not to hold them to the answer provided. Assistants need to ensure that they do not succumb to such pressure.

---

10. They should ask their dealer's compliance officer to explain the limits that pertain to a licensed assistant in that jurisdiction.

All team members must understand the limits of what they can do and must carry out their duties professionally. Here is an example: Mr. and Mrs. Evie are new clients. Mr. Evie intends to open an account for both of them. The signatures of both Mr. and Mrs. Evie are required for certain documentation and, therefore, Mr. Evie cannot sign for Mrs. Evie or vice versa. Furthermore, all decisions on Mrs. Evie's account must be appropriate for her and must be made based on her instructions. The same is true for Mr. Evie, who is told that he cannot sign the account-opening documents for Mrs. Evie; she must meet the advisor before her account can be opened. The contact information is completed for Mrs. Evie, along with her personal identification, but the balance of the information is left blank until she meets with the advisor. Mr. Evie tells the advisor that Mrs. Evie will call to arrange a meeting to complete and sign the documentation. The advisor does not hear from Mrs. Evie for several days and asks John, his licensed rookie, to call her to arrange an appointment. Mrs. Evie is very hard to reach and after several weeks, John becomes impatient. One day when the advisor is not in the office, Mr. Evie asks to speak to John. He tells John that Mrs. Evie is in Omaha visiting her sick mother. Mr. Evie tells John that Mrs. Evie has told him to complete the forms and sign for her. John allows Mr. Evie to sign for his wife and opens the account. Although the advisor never met Mrs. Evie, he begins trading on the account.

The rookie's failure to adhere to the office rules and, in this case, probably to the compliance regulations in the jurisdiction, exposes the advisor to a potential claim from Mrs. Evie if she loses money due to unsuitable trades. The fact that Mr. Evie signed the forms and that the advisor never met the client is evidence of the advisor's negligence and a good reason why Mrs. Evie may successfully argue that the forms do not reflect her personal risk and financial needs. Even the excuse that the advisor thought his rookie, John, had met with her is insufficient, because it is the advisor's responsibility, not the rookie's, to meet her: the advisor is responsible for the advice and, specifically, for the choice of investments for Mrs. Evie.

Setting the tone with the client and managing client expectations throughout the relationship is much more difficult if the advisor's team does not consistently follow the rules, particularly if those rules have been communicated to clients. Failing to follow the rules in these types of circumstances exposes advisors and dealers to lawsuits and regulatory complaints.

TEACHING OLD CLIENTS NEW TRICKS

Long-time clients may not be accustomed to the advisor's new professionalism. How do advisors help long-established clients adapt to new systems? The simple answer is, "Communicate, communicate, communicate." Advisors must explain how these new processes will help these clients and provide even better service than before.

Advisors try to persuade me that these new processes will scare clients away and, specifically, that clients will not like it when advisors take notes during meetings. To that I respond, "Balderdash!" I have taken notes in every client meeting, and a client has never (ever) complained about this. Besides, I wouldn't trust clients who object to my note taking.

Before advisors introduce new systems, they should be sure that their team members understand their respective roles and the way in which the new systems will operate. Again, when there is buy-in from staff, the new systems will be incorporated more smoothly.

If possible, advisors should introduce changes first to those clients they expect will accept them more readily. This will allow the advisor's team to work out the kinks before introducing the changes to clients less inclined to accept them.

When I coach advisors about setting rules early in the process to minimize exposure to client complaints, they inevitably think of several clients whose accounts are not managed according to my recommendations. The non-compliant advisors often sit quietly, beads of sweat forming on their brows. I tell them not to focus on their past infractions or on the fact that they did not set the rules with clients earlier. My advice is to focus on the present and future: clean up the office and staff practices. Get everyone operating professionally. Inevitably, advisors ask me, "But how can we teach all these old clients new tricks?"

I concede that it is more difficult to teach old clients new tricks, but with diligence, commitment, and support from staff, it is possible. Here are some suggested steps advisors can take to ease the pain for all concerned:

Step 1 — Review the client list and prioritize it according to the degree of risk exposure. The most exposure will be from the following types of accounts:

- large accounts—these clients have the most to lose and their complaints would result in the largest claims;
- accounts in which there is a significant proportion of higher risk investments and, therefore, a greater likelihood of loss;
- leverage/margin accounts—clients who lose money on borrowed money tend to complain the loudest as their losses go beyond their own capital;
- husband and wife accounts in which the advisor has not met one of the spouses;
- offshore accounts;
- accounts in which the advisor has not met the clients face to face;
- elderly clients with whom the advisor has never discussed power of attorney; and
- accounts in which the advisor takes instructions from the person with power of attorney, particularly those accounts belonging to clients whom the advisor has not met.

Step 2 — Advisors need to develop a plan that includes the help of their team members. The plan will vary depending upon the number of an advisor's clients and the amount of potential exposure to client complaints and lawsuits. Advisors need to contact each client individually. They need to ensure that any issue that puts them and their teams at risk is remedied. Advisors and their teams will not be able to remedy everything instantly, but this strategy will work if they develop a plan and system to review a certain number of clients monthly.

Step 3 — Advisors need to assess their staff. If they don't get support and "buy-in" from certain members of their teams, they may need to hire new people in their place. Advisors don't want the lax attitudes of apathetic staff to drag them down. They especially don't need the unnecessary, negative exposure that arises when a colleague doesn't share their goal to be in this business for long, but rather takes shortcuts to increase commissions. If a staff member shows little interest in compliance or in safer practices to protect the advisor's reputation, advisors must re-evaluate that staff member's role in the company.[11]

Step 4 — Advisors need to assess their clients. If they do not co-operate and an advisor thinks they are rogues,[12] he may want to cut them loose.

The advisor cannot expect to convert his office overnight. It takes time and commitment. Like most things, a compliant office is much easier to maintain once it is in good form.

Step 5 — Once the advisor is satisfied that her office is becoming more compliant and her clients have been trained, retrained, or terminated, then she can establish a follow-up plan to continue to improve efforts toward further compliance. This will include having better systems to maintain documentation and ensuring that her team continues efforts to comply. While no office can be perfectly compliant, advisors and their teams should aim for continual improvement.

SUMMARY

Professionalism is fundamental to the success of advisors and dealers. It is also important to communicate clearly with clients in order to manage their expectations. These expectations should be relayed early in the relationship. Effective listening and speaking skills and maintaining consistency in professional tasks are essential for managing client expectations.

---

11. The advisor will need to obtain legal advice in his jurisdiction to determine whether or not he will have to pay the staff member a sum to terminate the relationship, without further exposure to a lawsuit for wrongful termination, but this is beyond the scope of this book and as such will not be discussed.
12. See Chapter 7.

ADVISORS TAKE ACTION

✓ An advisor sells professional advice, which means clients must be made aware of available options and the main benefits and risks of each product and/or service.

✓ Effectively communicate to manage the expectations of both clients and advisors at the beginning of the relationship.

✓ Adopt systems that work best for you and your team. Consider using checklists and agendas for each client meeting and customize them for particular clients. Ensure that team members understand the systems and their respective roles.

✓ Once your office is compliant, establish a maintenance plan to ensure the office continues to operate in a manner that reduces risk.

CHAPTER 3
Know Your Client and Prove It

I. THE KYC FORM

What is the KYC (Know-Your-Client) form? It is a summary of essential facts collected by advisors about their clients. These facts are gathered to enable advisors to choose investments suitable to their clients' needs and risk tolerance. The information in the form is just a summary, however, and does not, by itself, prove that the advisor knew and understood the client.

The KYC form is simply one of many tools advisors use to fulfill ongoing regulatory and legal obligations to know their clients. The process begins when an advisor first meets the client and doesn't end until the account is closed.

The KYC form contains a summary of personal information about each client to guide the advisor and dealer and to ensure that the investments and insurance products chosen are suitable. But, from the beginning of the relationship, an advisor must know more than the basic information on the form. Further, throughout the period in which he or she advises the client, the advisor must know about any *changes* that may affect the client's objectives and risk tolerance.

Clients change with time. They get married, have children, get divorced, get married again, have more children, pay alimony and support, get jobs, lose jobs, get promoted, grow older, retire, resume employment after retirement, and so on. Their investment needs and goals change as their circumstances change. Accordingly, advisors have to continually ensure the KYC information is up to date so that accounts are attuned to their clients' current situations.

While properly completing the KYC form is a crucial step in the advisor/client relationship, maintaining an updated KYC form is just as important. Often when clients sue, the form supplied dates back to when the clients' circumstances were different. The form, therefore, does not reflect the

46

client's current objectives and risk tolerance. An outdated form can be evidence to support a client's allegations that the advisor was negligent. Courts have emphasized the importance of the advisor's obligation to respect the golden rule: know the client. The onus is squarely on advisors to ask clients for all relevant information.

Some advisors believe that completing the KYC form is a one-time event. In fact, the KYC questionnaire must be regularly updated. If the information on the form no longer reflects the client's current situation, the advisor and dealer may be seen as professionals who failed to fulfill their obligations. Advisors should update the KYC form whenever they become aware of clients' financial changes. While not all regulators specifically prescribe how frequently a KYC form should be updated, advisors should check with clients yearly to determine changes that may impact their financial situations.

II.   COMMON PITFALLS

Here are some common problems that arise through a review of the KYC form and that are likely to result in further investigation by a regulator:

CLIENT'S COPY DIFFERS FROM ADVISOR'S

Some advisors have been accused of having the client sign a blank KYC form, which they subsequently fill in themselves. The client later asserts that the KYC information is wrong. By maintaining notes of the conversations and steps taken to arrange for the signing of the form, the advisor should have evidence that the form was completed before the client signed it. Another good habit is to have clients date the document in their own handwriting, so that there is evidence of the date that they signed. This shows that the document was not merely dated by the advisor after the signature was obtained. The final KYC form should be delivered to the client so that there is no confusion about what is in the form that the dealer and advisor will rely upon.

THE ADVISOR NEVER MET THE CLIENT

Opening an account for a new client while relying exclusively on information obtained from an existing client can come back to haunt an advisor. For example, Mr. Smith wants his own advisor to open an account for Mrs. Smith. Mr. Smith insists that all information and instructions come from him. He says that although the account is under his wife's name, it is really his money; Mrs. Smith doesn't understand anything about finances and does not want to be bothered. What happens, however, if the advisor does not meet with Mrs. Smith and instead gets all his information about her from her husband? Simple—the advisor will be unable to meet legal and regulatory obligations if Mrs. Smith loses money in her account and issues a complaint alleging breach of the KYC rule, discretionary trading, and suitability issues. Why? Because the advisor, who never met or spoke to Mrs. Smith, did not gather sufficient information or know the client well enough to act responsibly on her behalf.[1]

Advisors tend to forget that even though the contact is an existing client, the ultimate client is the person under whose name the account operates. Even if the existing client has a power of attorney for the person under whose name the account is opened, advisors must ensure that they know new clients well enough to recommend suitable investments. Advisors must meet their duties by fulfilling KYC obligations with the named account holder. That way they can ensure that the account operates in accordance with the client's financial needs and risk tolerance. If advisors don't follow the above procedure, a much greater risk exists that, if sued or reported to the regulator by the client, the advisor will be unable to prove that he fulfilled KYC obligations.

There may be legitimate reasons for not meeting the client personally. For example, when a client is ill, the advisor may meet with the power of attorney, and sometimes advisors don't meet clients in person because the clients live far away. In most jurisdictions, rules or regulations do not prohibit the advisor from servicing the client by telephone, assuming the advisor is properly

---

1.   Meeting the client in person before opening the account is necessary, particularly to fulfill anti-money laundering (AML) obligations. The topic of AML is beyond the scope of this book.

registered in the client's jurisdiction and that the dealer's internal policies do not prohibit this kind of service. Some dealers may forbid it. Even when telephone service is permissible, I suggest that the advisor makes the effort to meet the client personally, early in the relationship. Advisors may find that they learn more about someone in person than on the telephone. When talking on the telephone, you cannot see body language, including eye contact, and you may not develop a true trust and connection.

ERRORS ON THE FORM

If numbers on the KYC form are added incorrectly, or if information is scratched out,[2] the form will not reflect well on the advisor as a professional. This may seem superficial but, even if a client's complaint has no merit, a small or inconsequential error may lead to a longer investigation by the regulator.[3]

THE CLIENT DISAGREES WITH INFORMATION ON THE FORM

Suppose Ms. Stevens' KYC form indicates that she accepts medium-risk investments. It also indicates that her income is between $75,000 and $100,000. Ms. Stevens later insists that she was risk averse and that her income was less than $75,000. While the production of tax returns can resolve the income issue, it is possible that during her meeting with her advisor, Ms. Stevens misstated both her income and her willingness to assume risk. In this scenario, it will be easier to prove that the form was consistent with the information imparted if the advisor has notes from the meeting confirming the discussion. Alternatively, if no notes were made during the meeting and the client asserts she signed a blank form, there may be very little chance the judge will take the advisor's word over the client's, particularly in light of tax returns confirming the client's evidence.

---

2. This is less of an issue with forms that are generated and completed by a computer.
3. In most jurisdictions, the supervisor/branch manager must also sign the KYC form before the account can be opened. Therefore, sloppy forms that pass through the system can also challenge and raise concerns about the supervisor's professionalism.

III. A CHECKLIST AND SUMMARY TO FULFILL THE KYC PROCESS

Advisors may find the following points useful in fulfilling the KYC process:

- Advisors should meet the client face to face before the account is opened, or make it a practice that in those limited situations where new clients are accepted over the telephone, they ensure a personal meeting is set up soon afterwards.[4]
- It is good practice for advisors to take notes that include as many points as possible about the client's background—before completing the KYC form.
- Advisors will want to insert something of significance in the "comment" section of the KYC form. A client will always provide information beyond the questions on the form. Such detail will show regulators and judges that advisors listened and were conscientious.
- Advisors should tell clients that if their personal situation changes, the investment plan must be adjusted. Advisors should ask clients to contact them and tell them when changes occur.
- A letter to clients, just to confirm there were no changes and to request that they contact the advisor if there are any, is recommended and is an annual regulatory requirement in certain jurisdictions.
- Each time the KYC form is updated, the advisor should send the client the KYC form that he or she signed and include a personal cover letter confirming the meeting.
- It is good practice for advisors to have a "tickler system" that brings each client's KYC form to their attention at least annually.[5]

---

4. In most jurisdictions, anti-money laundering laws mandate the identification requirements, but this is beyond the scope of this book.
5. The process of updating should be risk based so that advisors update more frequently in certain circumstances. Many dealers have an automatic letter that is delivered to clients annually to determine if the client has changed. Advisors should not, however, rely automatically upon such a letter, nor should they think that such a letter protects them from complaints alleging that they did not know a client.

Advisors can use the need to update the form as an opportunity to meet with clients. Advisors may find that they leave with a commitment to increase their portfolios or—better—with a check. Advisors should ask clients if they are satisfied with the relationship and if circumstances have changed at all. If a client is too busy to meet, a letter should be sent confirming that attempts were made to set up a meeting, along with a copy of the most current KYC form signed by the client to confirm that the information has not changed.[6]

- Advisors are obligated to inform themselves of any changes to clients' circumstances and to adjust the investments accordingly. If advisors document client files and a complaint arises, advisors can produce records to show that they knew their clients. If the investments are consistent with the KYC form, advisors will likely avoid penalties and bad publicity.

- Most KYC forms contain a clause, sometimes in tiny type, confirming that the client has received, read, understood, and agreed with the dealer's terms and conditions. These terms and conditions are usually set out on the reverse side of the form or in a separate booklet. While the client's signature confirms an intention to be bound by the terms and conditions, it will be difficult to enforce such terms if the client was never shown them and given an opportunity to read them before signing. It is good practice to explain, in advance of a client's signing, any of the terms that are particularly applicable to the client's contract. It is also important for the advisor to make a note of the following things: (1) that they discussed the terms and conditions, and (2) that the client was given an opportunity to read the terms and conditions before signing.

---

6. In some jurisdictions, regulatory requirements mandate the delivery of such letters periodically.

IV.   BEYOND THE FORM—
UNDERSTANDING CLIENTS

Please note that completing a single form neither fulfills the task nor proves to a judge that an advisor took the necessary time to get to know and understand a client. Almost every court case alleging unsuitable investments made by advisors turns on facts relevant to the client. For example, the client may assert that the money was intended for retirement.[7] The advisor may counter that he was never told that the money was intended for retirement but was instead told that it was "play money" for speculative investments. In an insurance case, the client may assert that he told the advisor he needed coverage for stored gas tanks on his property, but the advisor denies ever being told such coverage was necessary.

Learning the essential facts about clients is only the beginning. What is required to truly know a client? Since we have established that knowing your client means more than just completing a KYC form, what more must an advisor do to truly understand and later prove to a judge that he knew his client and that the investment and insurance products chosen were suitable? Advisors need to collect relevant facts about the client that go beyond the form.

Some advisors take comfort in simply obtaining the client's signature on the KYC form to confirm that the information on the form is reflective of the client. They avoid asking probing questions that go beyond the form for fear of offending the client. However, if advisors merely ask the questions on the form and avoid a full inquiry, they cannot obtain the answers necessary to fulfill their obligations. Furthermore, it is a mistake to merely give the form to the client to complete. The advisor must ask the necessary questions and use her professional abilities to review the answers and assess the client. Most clients are not equipped with the knowledge and education to complete the form. That is the advisor's job.[8]

---

7.   Anti-money laundering legislation will mandate the advisor to ask the client about the intended use of the account. The topic of AML is beyond the scope of this book.
8.   See p.38 of Thull's book, *Mastering the Complex Sale*: One should not assume ". . . higher levels of comprehension and decision-making ability on the part of . . . customers."

Here is a basic checklist of issues to review.
These issues go beyond what is on the form:[9]

- Past and Present Vocation—The form usually asks about the client's current job. But to really know the client, the advisor will also want to know whether he or she has had other business experiences, professions, or specialties.
- Past and Present Marital Status—If one only asks what the present status is, one will not know how many times the person was married. For example, if the advisor asks Mr. Stevens his present status, he may say separated or divorced. But if the advisor does not ask additional questions, she will not know how many times he has been married and divorced. Mr. Stevens may not want to volunteer this information, but it is important for the advisor to know.
- Past and Present Employer and Salary—The form likely only has a section for the client's present employer and salary. It is important, however, to know whether the client has occupied that position for long or whether he or she changes jobs frequently. Length of time spent at one job or switching jobs may affect the client's finances. This also applies to the section on the form pertaining to current income: it is necessary to ascertain whether income has been steadily increasing, decreasing, or remaining consistent. Furthermore, knowing the client's past position is important as it may provide the advisor with insight into the client's financial knowledge. For example, the client may say that his present position is in marketing but, unless asked, he may not reveal that his first job was accounting at one of the big accounting firms.
- Other Liquid Assets—The form provides for the client's present net worth but doesn't necessarily reveal her other assets and the amount of financial stability in her life.

---

9. This is a basic list. Advisors may want to explore these and other issues further.

- Wealth Accumulation—The form indicates the client's net worth but does not determine the source of the wealth. For example, has the client been a lifelong saver or is this a one-time inheritance?

Other questions related to the client's financial knowledge and sophistication will be explored later in this chapter.

If an advisor simply sticks to the form, there is little chance that he will gather the necessary information to know the client well enough and to prove to a judge that his version of the client's background information was accurate and that the investments were suitable.

Here is a sample of open-ended questions, in no particular order, which allow advisors to get to know their clients more thoroughly than is possible by just relying on the form.

To understand clients' financial obligations, stressors, and concerns:
- What do you like to spend your money on?
- What do you hate to spend your money on?
- What future financial obligations do you expect that concern you? What, if anything, have you planned to do about these obligations?
- What motivates or excites you in your job?
- What do you dream about and look forward to?
- What are your biggest regrets?
- What, if anything, holds you back?
- What, if anything, causes you stress/disturbs your sleep?

To understand clients' plans for retirement:
- What do you want to do when you retire?
- What current or future obligations, if any, do you have to take care of your parents? Spouse's parents?
- Until what age do you want to work in your present job?
- What work or hobbies will you have in retirement?
- What are your children's plans for education after high school?

The above lists are only samples. Other questionnaires, including those from mutual fund companies, may be useful. I recommend that advisors collect and review these questionnaires and choose the questions that are most useful in truly getting to know their clients. Remember, a single set of questions does not fit every client. Therefore, once advisors have prepared the questionnaire that they will use as a template, they must be flexible and be sure not to follow the questions as they would a script. Additional questions may be required.

V. HOW ADVISORS CAN PROVE THAT THEY TRULY KNOW THEIR CLIENTS

Since the advisor's version of events may be diametrically opposed to the client's version, how can the advisor prove that her version is the one a judge should favor? When neither the client nor the advisor took notes of their discussions, judges have been prone to sympathize with the version of events relayed by clients rather than by advisors. The advisor can change that by having a record of the facts provided by the client. A solid set of notes and records prepared by the advisor will help convince the judge that the advisor's version is the one to believe, especially since the client is unlikely to have any documentation to support his version.

VI. THE IMPORTANCE OF CONSISTENCY

Notwithstanding the tools used—questionnaires, forms, notes, tape recordings—the advisor must ensure that the responses noted in the KYC form or insurance application are consistent with answers provided by the client. For example, if an analysis of the answer in the questionnaire indicates that the client is risk averse, but other answers reveal that past investments were speculative, the advisor must ascertain whether past investments were unsuitable or whether the client has changed, and why. Simply following a strategy consistent with the client's past risk level will be insufficient to support a case that the investments were suitable.

VII. THE FIVE-STEP APPROACH FOR OVERWHELMED ADVISORS

Advisors who feel overwhelmed by this chapter can try this five-step approach to get them up to speed:

PLAN
Advisors can examine their client lists and prepare a schedule for the next several months. Assistants can help. Advisors should first choose the higher-risk clients, particularly those with whom they have not met for more than a few minutes over the past several years.[10]

CONTACT CLIENTS
Advisors should call each of their clients and tell them they want to take the time necessary to catch up with them.

GATHER INFORMATION
Advisors should simultaneously gather information from each client while creating an effective paper trail.[11]

CONSIDER OPTIONS
Advisors should consider the client's long-range goals and discuss options.

DETERMINE NEED TO ADJUST PRODUCTS
Advisors should ensure the existing products meet the client's newly-stated objectives and should adjust these products if needed, after getting the necessary instructions.

One year will probably have passed by the time advisors get through their entire client list. By then, advisors will be better able to invest additional funds based on comprehensive plans, client information, and proper instructions. This isn't something advisors can do quickly. They need to take their time to fix their mistakes before clients complain. The team should not be discouraged if this takes more time than expected.

---

10. For a list of higher-risk clients, see Chapter 2.
11. The issue of paper trails is explored in Chapter 6.

SUMMARY

KYC is a process that begins when advisors first meet clients and ends only when accounts are closed. KYC obligations are the basis for an advisor's professional liability. If used appropriately and consistently, KYC forms can assist advisors in fulfilling professional obligations and can guide them in choosing suitable products and investments for clients. Meeting with clients face to face, completing the KYC forms thoroughly, accurately, and regularly; recording all communications, and ensuring that clients confirm the information set out in the KYC forms are some of the ways that advisors can fulfill their obligations while practicing strong defensive strategies to avoid regulatory complaints or litigation.

ADVISORS TAKE ACTION

✓ Know your clients and meet with them face to face.

✓ Complete the KYC form accurately and ensure clients sign it.

✓ Continually update the KYC form and create a "tickler system" to help you do this.

✓ Keep notes of all communications and meetings with clients.

✓ Be consistent and employ strategies appropriate for the risk level of the client.

✓ Ascertain client sophistication and document accordingly.

✓ Always include comments in the comment section of the KYC form.

CHAPTER 4
The Suitability Challenge

The following is an example of a common scenario that creates big problems for advisors. Clara is 50-years-old and has been investing with an advisor for seven years. Her risk profile is medium, and she has a good understanding of securities from her years of investing with this advisor and previous advisors. She is not a high-risk investor and does not like to trade in securities that exceed medium risk. For this reason, her advisor suggested that Clara invest mostly in low-to-medium-risk mutual funds.

One day Clara calls her advisor, insisting that she invest in a particular fund or stock (depending on the license of the advisor). Clara had heard "through the grapevine" that this product is a "sure winner." The advisor quickly researches the investment and tells her it is speculative. Clara says that is fine. She instructs the advisor to sell some existing investments and buy her more speculative choice instead. The advisor follows her instructions, marking the trade unsolicited.[1] The advisor receives an e-mail from the compliance department alerting her that this trade is inconsistent with Clara's client profile on her KYC form. The advisor calls Clara and arranges for her to sign a new KYC form to allow for speculative investing worth 15% of her portfolio. Clara signs the updated KYC form. The investment improves and Clara is excited. She wants her advisor to sell more of her conservative investments and buy more of her speculative choice. The advisor remembers the previous exchange of e-mails with the compliance department and arranges for Clara to sign an updated KYC form that allows for speculative investments worth 50% of her portfolio. The advisor purchases more of the speculative investment for her, marking the trades unsolicited.

---

1.   See Chapter 4 for more on unsolicited/solicited trades.

I.   SUITABILITY AND THE KYC

The issue of suitability is the central focus of most claims and complaints against advisors and dealers. The same goes for insurance companies in regard to investment products wrapped in insurance policies. Upon examining the documentation, which includes the KYC forms for each of Clara's accounts in the past seven years, and with the help of Clara's lawyer, the regulator and/or judge will see that Clara's risk factors remained consistent for seven years. They will notice that it was only in the past year that the KYC was adjusted, not just once, but twice, to meet the risk factors of the new, speculative purchases, the ones in which Clara lost 35% of her portfolio.

Will these changes in the KYC form protect the advisor? Is the advisor vulnerable? What if the investment diminishes in value and Clara panics and tells her advisor to sell? Will the advisor and her dealer be in a good position to defend these trades before a regulator or judge? Can they prove these trades were suitable by producing the KYC forms? The simple answer is "no." In determining suitability, both the regulator and the judge look beyond the KYC form at the client, to determine her willingness and ability to assume the risk of each product.

II.   SUITABILITY AND PROOF

Closely connected to an advisor's obligation to know his or her clients is the concept of suitability. Advisors are required to ensure that investments fit the objectives and financial situation of each client. Courts and regulators charge advisors with the obligation of knowing the client and the product, and advising the client accordingly. Without supporting documentation that proves they fulfilled both of these obligations, advisors will be exposed to regulatory enforcement proceedings and clients' litigation claims.

A common misunderstanding among advisors is that a product is considered suitable if information on the client information or application form matches the trade—and that the application form can be adjusted accordingly. However, adjusting the client profile on the form to match the product risk often results in unsuitable investments.

That's because the client is ignored if the KYC form reflects the product and not the client. If the client profile changes, documentation beyond the updated KYC form must explain the reason for the change. While client changes will be discussed more fully in this chapter, here are some examples of evidence that might explain an increase in risk tolerance:

- Employment factors changed—Did the client receive a promotion at work and an accompanying increase in salary, or a bonus? Did her employer reach a milestone that renders the company more secure than when the client first opened her account?
- Financial situation changed—The client has recently inherited money or married someone with a secure job and substantial income. Or, the children have graduated from university and have secure employment (wishful thinking?), and the clients have more disposable income.
- Education and experience—The client may have taken a course or become more interested in the products. She may have started to browse the business section of the newspaper and has recently read books that analyze investing.

If, however, no documentation exists to support the change in the KYC form, but rather the form is adjusted merely to meet the risk of the investment, the investment is likely to be unsuitable. In Clara's situation, the advisor may have a problem as there is nothing to explain the changes.

The KYC forms are the initial and primary focus of judges, arbitrators, and lawyers. Their first review of the case includes a comparison of the investments and the KYC form to determine if the trades complained of are consistent with the client's stated risk factors and financial objectives. However, this is just the first step. The second step is determining whether documentary proof exists that the client's actual risk tolerance and objectives are reflected in the form. In other words, does the advisor have the evidence to support the information contained in the form? While Clara's risk tolerance may have changed, there must be evidence of this fact. If there is no evidence of what led to the change in risk tolerance, Clara's allegation that the investment was unsuitable may meet with success, even though the KYC form matched the trades. The accuracy of the KYC form is fundamental to a successful defense for the advisor, dealer, or insurance company. If the regulator or judge determines that the KYC form is wrong and, by that, I mean unreflective of the client, the advisor and dealer will likely end up paying to settle the matter. In addition, they may also be required to pay a substantial penalty to the regulator.

In teaching advisors what they must do to ensure that additional documentation supports the information on the KYC form, I use a chart called the Triangle of Suitability. By using the Triangle of Suitability, advisors can prove that the KYC form, particularly if adjusted, accurately reflects the client.

III. THE TRIANGLE OF SUITABILITY

Follow the three steps in the direction of the arrows:

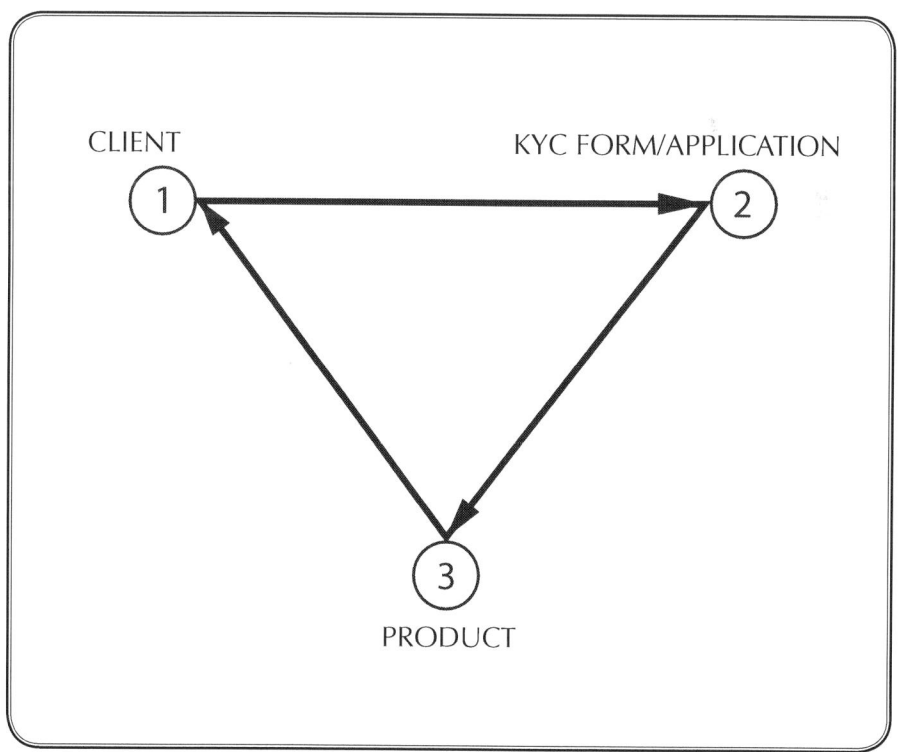

Step One is getting to know the client. Only after getting to know the client can the advisor move to Step Two and complete the KYC form or insurance application, which summarizes the information obtained in Step One. Products are then chosen according to what is outlined in the KYC form.

So, if we analyze what the advisor did in Clara's account, we will see that she didn't follow the direction of the arrows in the chart mentioned above. Instead, the advisor began with the investment, the third step, and worked in the opposite direction. The advisor adjusted the KYC form to reflect the product risk. This allowed the investment to pass the compliance review. Here is what was done:

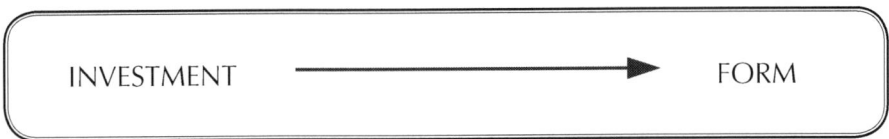

In Clara's case, she was no longer part of the equation. No questions were asked to document and explain the change in Clara's risk tolerance. It is unlikely, therefore, that the advisor could prove that the trade was suitable. If she loses money, Clara will turn to the advisor and the dealer alleging the investment was unsuitable. She will rely on her personal circumstances and investment history to prove that the speculative investment was too risky for her. To ensure investments are suitable, the advisor cannot leave the client out of the equation. Suitability is not whether the investment is consistent with the KYC form, but whether the investment is consistent with the client. Advisors can only defend themselves successfully if they can prove that the KYC form reflected the client at the time of the trade.

On several occasions, advisors have suggested to me that when the account is not in agreement with the client's profile, the compliance department sends them a message telling them to update the KYC documentation. Advisors have interpreted this to mean that the compliance department wants them to adjust the KYC form to meet the trades. I interpret this differently: compliance department staff may assume that the purchase is suitable but that the documentation has not yet been updated to reflect changes with the client. They may be reminding advisors to catch up with their documentation.

IV. SUITABILITY AND SUPERVISION

The advisor is the only person who can ensure that the Triangle of Suitability is followed consistently. The supervisor and the dealer's compliance department only review the KYC forms or insurance applications and products. They cannot ascertain whether the form reflects the client unless they have periodic client contact. Advisors generally loathe the prospect of supervisors directly contacting their clients. Advisors are worried that a call from the supervisor will raise concerns and reduce the client's confidence in the advisor. While this concern is understandable, a supervisor's appropriate and consistent contact with clients can protect the advisor and the dealer. Here are some ways to make the supervisor's inquiries seem more natural:

- When new clients meet members of the team, they should meet the supervisor, too. Explain to clients that the supervisor is another member of the team there to serve them. Of course, this is difficult if the supervisor is not in the branch every day.
- Show clients that the name and contact information for the supervisor and the assistant are on the periodic statements, if that is indeed your dealer's practice. Explain and note the fact that if clients have concerns, they should feel free to contact the advisor or the supervisor.
- Tell clients that at all times they have a right to inquire about any product and to challenge the advisor on any product. If concerns remain after the discussion, they can also use the supervisor as a resource.
- Tell clients that they will occasionally hear from all members of the team—the supervisor, the advisor, and the assistant. This way, a call from the supervisor seems routine.
- When they call, supervisors must ensure that they do so in a manner agreeable to advisors. Supervisors may need coaching in order to instill confidence in both clients and advisors and to avoid losing good advisors through such active supervision. I suggest that supervisors include advisors in any client calls. This allows supervisors to objectively listen to complaints,

without advisors feeling threatened that complaints are being handled behind their backs.

I use a method of supervision with members of my team. I delegate many of the files and the work on the files to lawyers in several offices my firm has across Canada. I consult with the clients in advance to explain why I am delegating the matter, so that they understand that it is for their benefit. In certain circumstances, much of the document review and organization can be done by a clerk or associate whose hourly rate is significantly less than mine, or there is someone else who specializes in the area of law required for the file. In firms like mine, with more than 700 lawyers, clients benefit by getting the appropriate lawyer for their files. My partner Paul Dempsey is a securities lawyer and his clerk Melle Riviera is an expert on regulatory registrations, an area with which I am unfamiliar. When a client needs advice in this area, I suggest they consult Paul and have Melle do the work. However, I always remain in touch with clients. If they come in to meet Paul, I pop into the meeting. If, to save the client money, I delegate the matter to any of my junior associates or clerks—Colin, James, Scott, Danielle or Stacey—I stay in touch with the associate and the client to ensure the matter progresses to the client's satisfaction.

It protects the advisor if a supervisor in the securities industry gets involved with clients from the beginning. This way clients are not surprised to receive a telephone call from the branch manager, who can corroborate instructions previously given by clients to the advisor. If clients know they can speak to the supervisor about any concerns, they are more likely to complain earlier than if they don't know where to turn. Earlier complaints can be beneficial because small matters get resolved instead of becoming major client concerns that are likely to go to the regulator or court. Furthermore, if the matter does result in a regulatory complaint or litigation, and the allegations are that the investments were unsuitable, two professionals can comment on the client's risk tolerance and sophistication to prove that the investments were suitable.

We have discussed the importance of ensuring that investments are suitable, but we need to explore further why this exercise is so very difficult, which is the topic of the next section of this chapter.

V. PRODUCT RISK—ART OR SCIENCE?

During my seminars, advisors rightly complain that assessing the product risk is not straightforward, and they often argue with compliance officers over the classification of risk. Is there an objective, scientific way to determine risk? The answer is no.

What is the advisor to do? Many securities come with a prospectus that describes the investment and the associated risks. These documents are public and readily available. Even if advisors disagree with what's in the prospectus, it is important to remember the persuasiveness of the written word. The judge, jury, regulator, or any other person judging the risk factors of an investment will likely give more credence to the prospectus than to the advisor's personal, presumably subjective, view. To limit an advisor's risk, I strongly suggest that advisors refer to the risk factors set out in the prospectus or other accompanying documents, which describe the product and product risk.

Advisors also complain that the risk changes occasionally, which may put the client's portfolio offside. This is absolutely a valid concern. However, the professional advisor is charged with ensuring the investments are monitored for this and other reasons, and if certain investments get riskier, the advisor must contact the client to explain the change and recommend the investment be sold if it is no longer suitable. Monitoring product risk and advising clients are services for which advisors are paid.

Let's look at an example. Nick is invested in the stock of Boltco Inc., a company that manufactures bolts for gasoline tanks. Boltco's stock performed consistently over the past decade. But with the increased popularity of electric vehicles and hybrids, Boltco's value has diminished significantly and the risk level has been increasing. The advisor calls Nick to tell him of the recent decline of Boltco, but Nick works for one of the large car manufacturing companies, and he lacks confidence in hybrid and electric cars. Nick refuses to sell, expecting the value of the shares to rebound. What is the advisor to do? He is concerned that the investment may no longer suit Nick's account, but the client refuses to sell.

The advisor must document that he contacted Nick recommending that he sell, and that Nick refused. A letter confirming this exchange will likely persuade a judge that the client was advised to sell and, by refusing, accepted the risks.

Is suitability an art or a science? I believe it is both. It is an art because judgment plays an important role. It is also a science because there are certain objective criteria, such as the prospectus, to ascertain the risk level of the particular investment.

VI. THE CONSTANTLY CHANGING ELEMENTS OF SUITABILITY

Scott Grant is a senior executive at a small but well-established company. He has been consulting an advisor for three years, trading often in speculative, small cap stocks. On January 8, Scott phones his advisor to say that he has made a new year's resolution. He is going to be 40-years-old next year, and he wants to force himself to be more conservative and save money for his future; what that means, he doesn't yet know. He asks the advisor for assistance, but the advisor's current business model is very aggressive.

The advisor suggests a more balanced approach, and refers him to a team member and colleague Noit All (pronounced: know-it-all), a more conservative advisor. Scott tells his advisor that he trusts him and insists that he continue to be his advisor. Flattered, the advisor agrees. The advisor adjusts the risk tolerance on Scott's KYC form to reflect his reduction in risk tolerance from high to medium and suggests that a certain sum be removed from his paycheck every month to be automatically placed in more conservative, long-term investments. Scott agrees and signs his updated KYC form.

Scott tells his advisor that he just received part of his annual bonus ($100,000) and wants to put that sum into his new, more conservative account. He also received a raise, so he would like to put an additional $1,000 into his new conservative account each month. He will have more than $112,000 in the new account by the end of the year. The advisor agrees that in the next year he will evaluate how much money he should put in at that time, depending on Scott's bonus. The advisor bounces this off his colleague, Noit All.

Noit All agrees but suggests in an e-mail that given Scott's current personal situation, the advisor increase the $1,000 to $4,000: Scott has a substantial income and few financial obligations. The advisor does not suggest this to Scott as he thinks that it would be too much for him given his expensive lifestyle.

The advisor suggests certain mutual funds and blue chip investments and Scott agrees. Again, the advisor bounces this off his colleague. Noit All e-mails the advisor again, suggesting that if Scott wants slow and steady, the funds that the advisor has chosen are too aggressive. The advisor disagrees because he knows Scott and thinks anything less aggressive will be too conservative. The money is delivered and the advisor deposits it into a new account for Scott—no margin, just a cash account. The advisor leaves his existing margin account open and the investments as they were when Scott approached the advisor in early January.

The market does not co-operate. The first monthly statement is delivered to Scott and he calls his advisor—the $100,000 he gave the advisor is now $82,000. He says he wanted slow and steady but moving up, not down. The advisor tells him not to worry; this is just a little blip. The next month goes by and he doesn't send his advisor the $1,000. The advisor doesn't want to bother Scott as he is a busy man, and the advisor figures he is waiting to see the investment increase in the next few months. The market, however, remains uncooperative and, over the following six months, the account diminishes further.

Meanwhile, Scott unexpectedly loses his job. Feeling very low, he is desperate to change something (everything) within the next few months before he turns 40. He thinks he has met the love of his life. He proposes to Pippi and she accepts. Pippi, being only 21, is the first of her group of friends to get married, and she wants a big ring and a wedding to match.

About 10 months after investing in what Scott thought were conservative investments, he calls his advisor asking for a check from the account, so that he can make a deposit for the ring and wedding. He doesn't tell his advisor that he has lost his job. When he discovers that the sum in his account has diminished, he is not happy. He asks about his other, more speculative, margin account and that one is down too.

Did The Advisor Get It Right?

- Did he explain the risks of the investments? No. He assumed that due to his client's experience and sophistication, he didn't need an explanation. Scott was sufficiently sophisticated that an explanation would not have been time consuming, and he and his advisor could have discussed whether the risk of the investments seemed appropriate, given his new outlook.
- Was this advisor best for this portfolio? While possibly equipped with the necessary skills to manage this more conservative portfolio, he wasn't interested in this area and lacked the patience to advise a client on this more conservative account. Perhaps then, the advisor should have insisted that the client obtain advice from Noit All or another advisor better equipped to manage this portfolio. Is it unrealistic to expect an advisor to insist on sending his client to a colleague who is better equipped to handle a certain account? Perhaps it is, but maybe this should change.
- Is there evidence in Noit All's e-mails that the advisor did not provide the client with investments to meet his long-term, conservative goals? Yes.
- Could Scott complain to the regulator? Yes. Every client has a right to complain to the regulator but, in this case, Scott may legitimately complain that his advisor failed to follow his instructions and that the investments were unsuitable.
- Is there evidence to support a claim? Yes. If Scott sues the advisor, the advisor will be required to give the regulator and Scott's lawyer all e-mails exchanged with Noit All.
- Did the advisor ignore the three elements of suitability (explained in the following section)? Yes.
- What are the three changing elements of suitability? The examples of Scott and of Nick, who invested in Boltco, confirm that three things always change:

1. Clients
2. Markets
3. Underlying Securities

CLIENTS CHANGE

As people grow older their circumstances change:

Relationships

People get married, have children, divorce, remarry, have more children, and blend families. Ultimately, their children may go to college or university; they may marry and have their own children. Lives change and financial needs change throughout this life cycle.

Jobs

In past generations, people remained at the same job for a long time, sometimes throughout their entire careers. Today, that's rare. Most people change jobs several times in their careers, and many people change careers altogether. Even those people who remain at the same company throughout their working lives can experience many changes. For example, the company may reinvent itself or merge with other companies. That's been the case in my own career. Although I have been at the same law firm since first becoming a lawyer, the firm has undergone many transformations: it has engaged in more than five mergers across Canada and has had several name changes.

Expectations

People's outlooks change over time. Among other things, expectations may touch on the following issues: finances, marriage, status, and other personal concerns. A change in expectations may herald a change in risk tolerance.

Values

People's values change over time. For example, they may value land and invest money in property. Then, they may value expensive cars and fancy watches. Later, they may treasure a high asset base, liquid or otherwise. It is, therefore, necessary to have regular client contact with open discussions of these changing values. That way, advisors can ensure investments are adjusted accordingly.

MARKETS CHANGE

While analysts are experts in what they do, they cannot accurately predict the future of our markets. The only predictable aspect of the markets is change. One day there may be a big demand for a certain product and the next day, no demand for it at all. With hindsight being 20/20, analysts can provide some logic to the shift. However, if anyone could predict these changes accurately, they could make themselves, and their clients, very rich. The difficulty is that clients sometimes have the unreasonable expectation that advisors can predict the future and that the commissions or fees they pay are in exchange for a guarantee that they will make money. Clients must be emphatically told that their advisor does not have a crystal ball. The advisor can evaluate and recommend suitable investment and insurance products and can explain the nature of each of these and their underlying risks. The client's obligation is to listen to what the advisor says, to ask questions to gain a better understanding, and to choose among the suggestions offered. If the client refuses to participate in the decision and asks the advisor to choose the investment, the advisor can say, "While I don't have a crystal ball, I think you would be well served with x, y, and z for the following reasons..." In such cases, documenting the due diligence and analysis of the products gives further credence to the advisor's recommendation.

UNDERLYING INVESTMENTS CHANGE

As in the example of Nick, who invested in a company called Boltco, demand for products can change without any notice. An entire industry can be affected by product change. Who could accurately predict the timing of the technology stock boom and bust? Management also changes, sometimes gradually and sometimes overnight. Labor issues can affect the productivity and profitability of a company. The cost of labor and products in the manufacturing process can also change a company's profitability.

VII. DIVERSIFICATION AND SUITABILITY

Advisors' intentions are honorable. They want their clients to succeed in the market and are tempted to sell products in the client accounts that are not doing well and to put the money into investments that will presumably do better. While this is what clients pay their advisors to do, advisors, egged on by their clients, can make the mistake of getting carried away or influenced by their clients, who are sometimes motivated by greed. It is one thing to transfer money from an investment that is not doing well to another that is doing better, but the advisor must be absolutely certain that the client account is not over-concentrated in any one security or industry. Failing to diversify a client's account leaves both the client and the advisor vulnerable. Clients who lose money in a sector or particular investment and who can prove that the advisor failed to adequately diversify their holdings may have cause for action against the advisor. For this failing alone, advisors may be held liable for losses.

Another common dilemma for advisors is when clients want to buy a product that the advisor wouldn't recommend to the client, because it is not one the advisor follows; the product is too risky; or the purchase might over-concentrate the account. When I have suggested that the advisor direct his client to open a self-directed discount account, some advisors have responded that such an option is impractical, asserting that time is generally of the essence, and if the advisor refuses the trade and the investment improves in value, it could come back to haunt the advisor. While this may be true in certain circumstances, I find that clients who push the advisor hard for improper purchases in their accounts tend to do so regularly. When advisors allow clients to buy inappropriate investments, advisors may find they are on a slippery slope, because the client-advisor relationship falls into a pattern of clients pushing the advisor to over-concentrate the account and buy too much of a single product. Often the advisor is lulled into a false sense of security, believing that the client must know what he wants. Before the advisor realizes what has happened, however, the pattern gains momentum and a life of its own. If the investment tanks, the client does not hesitate to argue that the advisor should have protected him from himself. Advisors in this predicament turn to me, exasperated, saying: "But that is what the client wanted."

VIII. UNSOLICITED TRADES

Sometimes, when a client account becomes over-concentrated, I ask the advisor whether the trades were "unsolicited." Typically, I receive one of the three following answers, each fraught with problems:

- "I marked every trade unsolicited." The advisor, not understanding why and in which circumstances trades are marked unsolicited, marks every trade unsolicited, thinking it will protect him. How, then, will the advisor prove that the trade in question was indeed unsolicited? The short answer is that he cannot. The advisor's credibility on this point is shot unless, of course, he has detailed notes of conversations with his client to prove that this particular investment was indeed unsolicited.
- "I never marked them unsolicited, but I know this one was!" In such circumstances, it will be the client's word against the advisor's, which is a difficult battle for the advisor to win.[2]
- "I was inconsistent. I didn't always mark trades unsolicited when the client initiated the purchase, but I never would have recommended this one." Again, with no paper trail, it will be the advisor's word against the client's.

These responses do not help the advisor who lacks a paper trail. It is important for advisors to determine what the regulatory framework is within their jurisdiction and to ensure that their strategy accords with that framework and is consistently applied. One of the best and, by that I mean, most credible, explanations advisors can provide is as follows:

"I don't specifically remember this trade or series of trades, but my regular business practice is to mark trades unsolicited that are initiated by my clients and to keep regular notes from telephone calls, in which I warn clients of the risks of the product, and the danger of over-concentration. You see, I read this boring compliance book years ago, and I adjusted my practice accordingly. I can refer you to the part of the book that I read and the handwritten (or computer) notes that I generated as a result."

Well, I know this is wishful thinking on my part, but I believe that advisors are moving toward this practice. The answer in the paragraph above is supported by three sources of evidence:

1. the advisor's regular practice;
2. the specific trades having been marked as unsolicited, which is indicated in the statements delivered to the client; and
3. the advisor's notes of his calls with the client.

---

2. The issue of credibility is explored in Chapter 6.

Depending on the legal and regulatory framework in advisors' jurisdictions, advisors can protect themselves when trades are over-concentrated or unsuitable, by properly marking unsolicited trades and by having a paper trail that documents warnings given to the client.

SUMMARY

Suitability is central to virtually all complaints lodged against advisors by their clients. Advisors are required to ensure that every investment accords with the objectives and financial situation of every client. Understanding the complexity and meaning of suitability, learning the three steps of the Triangle of Suitability, and appreciating how suitability is both an art and a science can help advisors properly gauge investments to ensure that any investment is properly suited to the particular client.

ADVISORS TAKE ACTION

✓ Ensure that client changes are reflected in notes when the risk tolerance on the KYC form changes.

✓ The KYC form must reflect the client, not the trade (the Triangle of Suitability).

✓ Have an objective, red-flag process (science) and apply judgment (art) to assess the product risk.

✓ Keep your eye on the three changing elements of suitability—an advisor's biggest challenge—and adjust accordingly.

✓ Ensure that each account is properly diversified and that trades are correctly marked unsolicited, with documentary proof for support.

CHAPTER 5
Know Your Product and the Risks

Professional advisors are obligated to explain the dangers and risks associated with the products they sell—and not just the positive attributes. Advisors need to appreciate the importance of explaining to clients the risks associated with each product they sell. Here are some of the excuses advisors give to rationalize not explaining the risks—and some of the problems associated with relying on any of these excuses.

I.   "THE CLIENT WOULDN'T UNDERSTAND EVEN IF I EXPLAINED IT"

Advisors who have unsophisticated clients are correct to assume that these clients may not understand the risks of the products. The problem with that reasoning, however, is that judges tend to sympathize with unsophisticated clients who purchased products without wholly comprehending their risks. Judges pay close attention to evidence relating to what was explained about the risks of the product before it was purchased and to steps taken by an advisor to satisfy himself that the client truly understood and accepted the risks.

No doubt, an unsophisticated client and some sophisticated clients will allege that the advisor didn't explain the risks. The advisor must have evidence that the risks were explained in a manner that the client understood and that the client accepted those risks. If a client is that unsophisticated and the product that complex, the advisor must evaluate whether this product should be sold to this client.

Indulge me while I use a crazy analogy from a Jerry Seinfeld television episode. In one episode, Jerry is out for dinner, where he is introduced to his friend's girlfriend. She speaks so quietly that he cannot hear her. In fact, he refers to her as the "low talker." At dinner he tells her he is going to be a guest on an evening talk show. Since he cannot hear her, Jerry simply nods and agrees politely to everything she says throughout dinner, including her request that on the show he wear a "puffy shirt" she designed that resembles a white pirate shirt. I like to use this little story because Jerry didn't know what he was agreeing to. He didn't realize that he had actually agreed to appear on national television dressed like a pirate. While not a perfect analogy, this story shows that, like Jerry, clients may agree to things they don't understand. Clients who don't understand a product's risks don't know what they are agreeing to buy. It might follow that people who do not understand what they have agreed to, have not actually agreed to buy the product at all. Put another way, if people do not fully appreciate the risks they may not have agreed to buy it in the first place. This is particularly so since the advisor selling the product has the duty to fully understand the risks and explain them to clients in such a way that they understand, before they decide what to purchase.

In fact, it is explaining the risks, as well as the other attributes of the product, that distinguishes an advisor from a salesperson selling a suit. The judge may believe that a client didn't understand the complex language used or what he or she was buying. The judge may, therefore, order the advisor to reimburse the client for losses. That is the risk advisors take when selling clients investment or insurance products that they didn't fully explain.

The advisor must:

- understand the product,
- explain the product,
- have the evidence to prove that an explanation was provided, and
- have the evidence to prove that the client understood the explanation and accepted the risks of the investment, or the limitations or exclusions of the insurance policy.

Doctors must explain the risks of certain drugs or surgery before the patient takes the medication or goes under the knife. Lawyers must explain the risks of certain alternatives such as if we go to court you could lose and be obliged to pay the plaintiff piles of money; while, if you settle, the matter will not be public as it would be if you went to court. Before they sell products to clients, advisors, like other professionals, must explain to clients the risks, limitations, and exclusions of these products. How can advisors ensure that they have the necessary evidence to prove that they explained the risks?

Advisors can do any or all of the following:

- Take notes of what is discussed at the meeting with the client, which can be an arduous, but necessary, task.
- Tape the conversation, but this may offend the client and be costly to transcribe or store in a way that can later be retrieved.
- Use an agenda with boxes to tick off what has been explained, and get the client to sign at the bottom.
- Use the prospectus, which describes the type of person who should invest in the product and the risks involved. An advisor would open the prospectus to the applicable pages and read them to the client or summarize them and note the pages and paragraphs that were reviewed. While in many circumstances this may be impractical, it's fairly easy to do when meeting the client in person. The advisor can take the copy of the prospectus, fold the pages describing the risks, and make a note of having explained the relevant sections of the prospectus to the client. This provides further support for an advisor's version of events.
- Help clients understand their role. Advisors should tell clients it is important that they find one place to keep all the materials they get in the mail or at advisor-client meetings, so that they can easily refer to this information. Advisors should also tell clients to call with any questions. In fact, helping the client to organize investment materials can be a promotional opportunity for advisors. For instance, advisors can give clients an accordion file or binder every year in which to put all materials given to them. The outside of the file or binder can feature the advisor's name, company logo, and the year. Not only does such a file or binder help clients remain organized, it also protects the advisor when the client claims that he did not receive any materials from the advisor. The advisor has a note that he sent the client an accordion file each year, and

the files in the advisor's office show that the materials were delivered. Even if the client trashes the material he received from the advisor, the advisor can prove that he sent the client information to help him help himself. Furthermore, some of the material that advisors send clients may also be required by their accountants to prepare tax returns.

Advisors who ensure that clients keep all these materials are helping to protect themselves if a client decides to sue. A litigious client will show his or her lawyer all the information and documentation provided by the advisor and may inadvertently convince a lawyer, particularly one working on a contingency basis, that this is not a case she can win. Let me explain. In some jurisdictions, lawyers are permitted to be retained by clients on the basis that the lawyer receives a portion of the proceeds from any settlement or judgment. Therefore, the lawyer working on a contingency basis assesses the likelihood of the plaintiff's success before accepting a retainer. If the lawyer thinks success is likely, she would be more inclined to take the case. Otherwise, she may refuse the retainer, and the client will have to convince another lawyer to take the case. This may discourage the client from suing.

Advisors will win more than half the battle if they can prove that they explained the risks. But the most difficult hurdle is proving that clients actually understood or had the capacity to understand the risks that were explained. Advisors cannot crawl into clients' brains during a meeting or telephone call to know if they are just saying they understand or whether they actually do understand the product and associated risks. However, advisors can acquire certain subtle pieces of evidence to assist them in proving that clients understood the risks:

- Did the clients ask questions that reflect their level of understanding? If so, advisors should write down the questions, word for word and in quotations if possible, as this will be evidence that clients understood. Silent clients who glaze over and nod their heads when asked if they understand the product and the risks may be the most dangerous clients, and advisors will have the most difficulty proving that they had the capacity to understand the risks and that they understood them.

- Advisors should ensure that they have a history of the types of investments the clients invested in or the insurance products obtained in the past, especially those purchased from another advisor at another company. If the current advisor recommends the same products or those similar in type and risk to those the client had in the past, the advisor is better equipped to prove that clients were sufficiently experienced to understand the risks. It can be more challenging to convince a judge that the client understood the risk of the product if it is different in attributes and risk level than products previously purchased. If clients want to buy products that differ in attributes and risk level from those previously purchased, advisors should pay closer attention to their explanations of the product's attributes and risks, and ensure the client understands. Advisors also need to ensure their notes reflect their explanations.

- Advisors should ask the clients questions to determine their level of understanding. For example, a client who moves to a riskier product based on the advisor's recommendations can be asked what she understands about the risks associated with the product she previously invested in. Then an advisor can ask a client what she regards as the source of increased risk in the type of product the advisor is considering for her. The conversation can go something like this:

Advisor: "Miss Teak, in the past, you invested in mutual funds that had a substantial equity component. What did you perceive to be the level of risk in that type of investment?"

Miss Teak: "I thought there was some risk because we looked at the prospectus and it confirmed that there would be some volatility with the underlying equities in the funds."

Advisor: "So now we are considering the prospect of investing in some shares of blue chip corporations. What do you understand about that specific risk?"

Miss Teak: "Actually I thought it was more or less the same risk because the mutual funds I was in were all equity based. Now I am just going to be concentrating on fewer companies."

Advisor: "Actually, what you say is true. You will be putting your money into fewer companies; however, with that move, you introduce more risk. Do you understand why?"

Miss Teak: "Oh I see. If I concentrate on fewer companies then I am putting more of my eggs into fewer baskets." [Note: advisor should write this down!]

Advisor: "Yes, that's exactly true. The mutual funds enable you to invest in several companies with one investment, and the shares are only in a few companies. How do you feel about taking on that additional risk?"

Miss Teak: "How much additional risk is it, do you think?" [Note that this is the question the advisor will want to write down word for word as it confirms that Miss Teak understands she is taking on additional risk by moving from mutual funds to shares of individual corporations.]

Advisor: "You were taking a low amount of risk with the mutual funds you invested in until now. If we keep you in blue chip stocks, I'd say you would take on medium risk, depending on the particular investments."

Miss Teak: "I am comfortable with medium risk, but I would not want to take on a high risk. Also, as long as the investments are in blue chip companies and I am investing in several of those companies, I am okay. I will want to review each prospectus in advance to discuss your suggestions." [The advisor should write down this answer too.]

Advisor: "That's great. I will send you a package next
week with each prospectus, and I will place a
Post-it® Note on the pages that I think will help
you understand the risks. Feel free to review the
entire prospectus, and call me with questions
so that we can decide which investments to
buy. In the meantime, we will need to review
each of the mutual funds to determine whether
there are any redemption costs associated with
liquidation and which, if any, you want to
liquidate or whether you want to wait."

It is much easier to take notes when others speak than when we speak
ourselves. However, if advisors can take some notes while speaking, it
will help them prove that they explained the risks. At the very least, they
should jot down the following notes from what Miss Teak said. They can
do so in their own abbreviated style.

Miss Teak

- wants stocks rather than funds;
- knows there is more risk with stocks;
- understands "concentrating" on fewer companies than mutual
  funds;
- knows "more eggs in fewer baskets" increases risk;
- asked "How much more additional risk than mfs?"
- says med, fine; not high risk—stick with blue chip and wants
  prospectus for each before investing.

These basic notes will make a big difference if the client, having
never before invested in stocks, loses her shirt on a bad run and decides
to sue the advisor for the losses.

What if the client is not like Miss Teak and neither speaks about
nor indicates her understanding or acceptance of the increased risk?
The simple answer is, regardless of whether the client is switching
product type or remaining within the same product type, if she doesn't
understand and accept the increase in risk, the advisor should not put

her in that product. Even if the advisor believes that her portfolio will benefit from some movement, if the client doesn't engage in discussions sufficient for the advisor to later prove that she understood and accepted the additional risk, the advisor should not convince her to change to a riskier product. The advisor does not want to be responsible for the client's potential losses. Remember, the client's signature on a KYC form is unlikely to be enough to convince the regulator or judge of her change in risk tolerance. The advisor should not avoid providing the client with an explanation, and then rationalize doing so by saying that the client wouldn't understand: it is the precise duty of a professional advisor to explain the options and associated risks. If the client doesn't understand, it clearly indicates that either the advisor has not explained the product sufficiently or that the product is too complicated for the client.

II. "THE CLIENT WOULDN'T BUY THE PRODUCT"

Many advisors worry that if their clients understood the risks of a certain product, they would not invest in it, and the advisor will lose the sale. The problem with this mentality is that the advisor is thinking like a salesperson rather than a professional. A professional advisor can sell a product only after the client understands and accepts the risks. If, after an explanation of the risk factors, a client does not buy the product an advisor recommends, an advisor should consider himself lucky. If the client had bought the product without understanding the risks, he might later pursue the advisor for reimbursement of any losses. With the vast array of products available in today's market, if a client finds one product too risky, the advisor can recommend others more suited to the client's risk tolerance.

Sometimes advisors are so keen about a particular product, they recommend it to all of their clients. The product may be attractive to the advisor because of the commission, but advisors must be very careful not to choose products for clients based on their payout. This would be a conflict of interest because the advisor may be perceived as putting his personal interests ahead of his clients' interests. This could lead to litigation by groups of clients by class action or otherwise. They may all seek reimbursement for their losses in the investment. When advisors believe they have identified a real winner, they must be disciplined enough to sell it only to those clients with the appropriate profile and risk tolerance.

III. "I CAN'T EXPLAIN THE PRODUCT"

If advisors cannot explain a product, it may be because they don't really understand it. Before recommending a product, advisors must thoroughly understand it. For example, if it is a common share, advisors will need to do some basic due diligence. This may include a review of recent press releases, the annual report, newspaper articles, a review of senior management, and any analyst reports available. Advisors need to be careful, however, not to rely too heavily on analyst reports to sell the product. While analysts are very useful, they cannot predict the future and cannot know with certainty what could happen to the stock. Advisors should read everything available and then use their own experiences and judgement to decide whether this is a good product to recommend to the client. After all, clients assume that advisors know about the company before they recommend it. The clients will assume, and judges and arbitrators will expect, that advisors have collected the necessary information and analyzed the product attributes and risk before making recommendations. In addition, common sense should dictate that if a trained financial services professional can't understand a product, most likely, her clients will not understand it either.

If it is an insurance product, advisors should ensure that they understand the application and exemptions sufficiently to explain them to clients. Advisors should also understand how the products they offer differ from each other.

If a product is more complex or the advisor is less familiar with the product or product type, it is much more work. Of course, advisors must be sure they have the necessary license to sell any product. Presumably, dealers only allow advisors to sell products they have licenses to sell. But, unfortunately, some advisors have been told by outside suppliers of products that they can sell them off the dealers' books (commonly referred to as "off-book transactions") or by referring the client to the supplier and getting a share of the fee or commission. Depending upon what the product is and how it is sold, such sales may contravene the local securities laws and regulations. If advisors are unsure whether the product is one that they are permitted to sell or whether the referral arrangement proposed complies with local laws, they should ask compliance officers and/or their legal support team before engaging in any such arrangement. ComplWWiance and legal staff will tell advisors whether the product or transaction is permitted and how to structure or process the sale to protect the advisor and his or her dealer and client. If the compliance and/or legal team counsel the advisor not to engage in such transactions, I strongly suggest advisors listen. Non-compliance may lead to termination and loss of license. In most jurisdictions, advisors are obliged by regulation and internal company policy to advise their dealers if they engage in outside business activities. Advisors considering selling off-book products, even if completely unrelated to the securities business, are obliged to first advise and get permission from their dealers.

Finally, if the product or product type is new, advisors should read all the available information and attend seminars to educate themselves and, of course, advise clients if the product lacks a track record in contrast to other products clients can choose.

If the product is complex, advisors may want to prepare charts, diagrams, or memos to help explain the product to clients. The rule of thumb is if advisors cannot explain the product, then they do not understand it well enough to sell it.

Regardless of the type or complexity of the product, advisors will want to ensure that they document all due diligence so that they can later prove that they had the necessary information to properly assess and understand the product.

IV. "THE CLIENT WILL BUY WHATEVER I TELL HIM TO BUY, SO WHY WASTE EVERYONE'S TIME?"

Clients commonly tell advisors not to waste everyone's time explaining the product and the product risk. Advisors who heed this suggestion expose themselves to significant risk. These are exactly the types of clients—those who are not prepared to invest the necessary time to understand the products—who come back to bite advisors with a lawsuit alleging the very thing they told advisors not to do. That is, they complain that advisors never explained the product or the risks. Advisors who allow their clients to lull them into a false sense of comfort expose themselves to the dangers of the passive-aggressive and super-aggressive clients discussed in Chapter 7.

Clients who understand the product and the risks are less likely to launch complaints, because their expectations have been properly managed. Furthermore, if the advisor has evidence that the product and risks were explained, a disparaging client is less likely to succeed in launching a complaint. Advisors must prepare clients for the risks. By explaining the risks, by reviewing the prospectus, press releases, and other public documentation, and by ensuring that the client's risk tolerance and financial objectives accord with the products, advisors will avoid putting themselves in the position of guarantors.

Very often professionals ask me, as a lawyer, how I handle my clients in similar circumstances. The answer depends on the particular case—what a typical (unhelpful) lawyer's answer! There may be situations in which I believe one route is far better for the client than any other, and I will explain my view to the client. However, when the choice is not as clear-cut, I attempt to persuade clients to decide, with my support, because they must live with the choice. Either way, I do not allow clients to delegate the decision-making to me. When one encourages clients to decide, they are more likely to become engaged in the process and to make an effort to understand the choices and risks. Clients should understand that they have so much vested (or invested) that it is important that they sufficiently understand the options, risks, and rewards in order to make an informed decision. Such an exercise will also help manage their expectations.

Advisors can also help clients take responsibility for their choices by explaining that it is the obligation of clients to review the periodic account statements they receive. Clients may say they haven't reviewed statements from their previous advisors because they didn't understand them. This is an advisor's opportunity to distinguish herself from the client's previous advisor by explaining the statements as often as necessary to ensure that the client fully understands his investments and their progress. If the advisor explains the importance of reviewing the statements and makes a note that she explained both the importance and the actual layout of the statements, and the client still ignores his mail, the advisor is more likely to appear professional and the client negligent.

An advisor needs to tell a potential client that there is a prerequisite for becoming one of her clients: to qualify as a client, the person must take the time to ensure that they understand the products and their risks. Clients must understand that investing or buying insurance products involves a considerable investment of their own time and energy. Advisors need to let clients know that if they cannot invest this time and energy, they need to find a different advisor. This is a hard message for advisors to deliver, particularly when faced with a wealthy client who does not want to take the time. Letting such clients go hurts an advisor's bottom line in the short run. However, such clients can be a major liability in the long run, as they have the resources to commence legal action against advisors and dealers. Advisors must assess the risks and make their own decisions about whether to work with such people.

Advisors should not say they are wasting everyone's time, thereby excusing themselves from their obligation to explain the product and its risks. Advisors who do shrug off their obligation this way may be held to be the guarantor of their clients' losses.

SUMMARY

It is very important for both advisors and clients to understand the products and the risks associated with them. One would think that clients would want to make an informed decision regarding their money and, as such, would want to understand the underlying nature of their investments. However, this is not always true. Advisors should, therefore, employ defensive strategies and comply with their duty to inform clients about the products or investments being considered, as well as the related risks. In a litigation context, judges tend to be less sympathetic to the advisor, the "sophisticated" professional. Advisors who ensure that their clients understand the products and accept the risks make it less probable that clients will lodge complaints. Even if they do complain, there is less chance that such advisors will be held responsible.

ADVISORS TAKE ACTION

✓ It is the advisor's obligation to understand the product and the risk factors associated with the product.

✓ Explain the risk of products and ensure that clients understand these risks.

✓ Keep records of all communications.

✓ Ask questions to determine clients' levels of sophistication and keep accurate records of these communications.

✓ Inform clients of their obligation to review the periodic statements they receive regarding their investments.

✓ Let the client ultimately decide whether or not to purchase the product.

CHAPTER 6
How to Win the Credibility Battle

I. SOPHISTICATION

Advisors are lulled into a false sense of security when clients arrive at their offices for the first time, asserting that they are sophisticated investors. Their expensive clothes, watches, or cars support the advisor's superficial assessment of such clients. When advisors are sued by these same clients, they are puzzled by the demand letter and subsequent claim that describes the client as unsophisticated and vulnerable. Advisors turn to me and say that the client is knowledgeable and sophisticated. The problem lies with the lack of evidence. These advisors have nothing other than mere superficial impressions. The advisor says repeatedly, "But I know he is sophisticated." While the client may very well be sophisticated, unless and until I, the lawyer, have concrete evidence, the advisor's general impression does not assist him in his defense.

Let me describe one advisor who retained me and insisted that the client suing him was indeed sophisticated, even though he had no evidence to prove it. I filed the defense on the advisor's behalf, asserting that the client was sophisticated, but I had no particulars supporting the statement. I proceeded with my examination (deposition) of the client, which the advisor's lawyer is entitled to do in most jurisdictions. As a matter of course, in the first five minutes of the examination, I asked the client about his educational background. I learned that he had taken the necessary courses to become an advisor years before but never followed through. At that point, I stopped the examination and asked the complaining client to leave the room so that I could have a discussion with the opposing counsel.[1] I explained that the

---

1. In this case, the opposing counsel was not well enough versed in this area of law or industry to comprehend the implications of his client's answer. There are, however, many other very experienced lawyers who represent complaining clients in the industry.

client certainly understood each investment and the associated risks and that whatever the client didn't understand was his own fault, because he did not review the materials provided at the time of investing or the materials delivered thereafter. The matter was ultimately abandoned by the advisor's client. Nevertheless, the advisor and dealer had to pay me a significant sum in legal fees just to get to that stage in the proceedings.

One of the risks for advisors and dealers is that clients win judges' sympathies by saying that they were unsophisticated and relied exclusively on their advisor when purchasing investment and insurance products. In reviewing the reasons judges give for their decisions, one usually sees references to the relative sophistication of the client and the advisor. The theory is that the poor uneducated client, who knew nothing about investment and insurance products, relied upon the educated, knowledgeable, and experienced advisor, and the result was unsuitable investments and losses.

If sophistication is so important, why don't advisors take the time to collect the necessary information to defend themselves against clients who are prepared to proclaim just about anything—including their own ignorance—in order to get their money back? The short answer is, advisors haven't received enough explanation and information to appreciate the importance of sophistication and how it can determine who wins the credibility battle. Yet the issue of the client's sophistication with respect to the product he buys may be crucial to the advisor's successful defense.

In order to develop a paper trail to support an advisor's contention that the client is sophisticated, what should advisors ask clients in the first meeting? Here is a checklist:

EDUCATION

Does the client have a post-secondary education—a college or university degree, courses, or certifications of any kind? What is the client's educational level, including area of focus in university or college?

READING

Which newspapers or magazines does the client subscribe to or read regularly? In particular, does the client follow business news on TV and/or in the newspapers? Does she know how to follow stocks in the newspaper?

TYPES OF ACCOUNTS
What types of accounts has the client had in the past— margin accounts, discount accounts, discretionary accounts with a portfolio manager?

INVESTMENT DECISIONS
How has the client made investment decisions with previous advisors? Has the client ever suggested investments, insurance products, or strategies to previous advisors?

PAST VOCATION
As stated earlier, although most advisors ask clients about their present occupation, it also helps to know what the client's previous jobs were. As baby boomers age, many of them no longer work full time, and more of these clients take odd jobs or are retired. If the only information collected is about a client's present occupation, the advisor will not know, for example, that the client was previously a comptroller of a company. Such information would definitely support the assertion that the client was somewhat sophisticated— she understood numbers and presumably would have understood the statements and prospectus information delivered.

BALANCE SHEET AND INCOME STATEMENT
Does the client know how to read balance sheets and income statements? Has he ever done this at work?

INTERNET
Does the client know how to check her stocks on the Internet?

In gauging a client's sophistication, there are other questions and areas to explore. Perhaps advisors can think of a few such questions to add to their lists.

Armed with this information in a paper or electronic file, advisors will no longer be vulnerable to clients who say they didn't have any idea what the products were or that there was any risk that they could lose money. This information will also help advisors assess in what detail they should explain the characteristics and the risk of the products they recommend.[2]

What is the credibility battle? We explored the risk to credibility in Chapter 1. The anecdote about Mac, the advisor, and his client, Mr. Kirk, illustrated the danger of a judge or arbitrator tending to believe the client's version of events over the advisor's version. What is often a judge's greater sympathy for clients is partially based on the perception that clients know less than and are more dependent upon professionals of all kinds, including the advisor in the securities and insurance industry. In addition, professionals of all kinds, including advisors, are expected to have proof supporting their version of events. Without such proof, the advisor's most valuable assets are challenged: reputation, license, and money.

II. ENHANCING CREDIBILITY

Advisors say that their clients will not regard them as professionals if they take notes during meetings. Advisors are concerned that if they take notes, it will appear to clients that the advisor is not listening to them. I believe the opposite is true. Indeed, most other professionals take notes while meeting with clients, and they are not accused of being unprofessional or not listening. When I went to meet my advisor for the first time, he sat back and just talked to me. He then attended one of my seminars and asked me why I didn't tell him to take notes during our meeting. I teased him that when I come to see him, I am paying him for his advice. If he wants to come and see me and pay me for my advice, he can book an appointment. We had a laugh.

Advisors also worry that their notes will come back to haunt them, because if they write something down, it can be misconstrued, or if the notes are incomplete, it will get them into more trouble than a blank page and a "my word against theirs" stance. I suggest that advisors are the best interpreters of their own notes, and their oral evidence will close the gaps.

---

2.   The issue of product risk is explored in Chapter 5.

Professionals take steps to protect themselves and to ensure their version of events is believed. Doctors and dentists maintain written charts for each patient, recording the date of the appointment, the subject of discussion, and the advice given. It has become a running joke that you need bad handwriting to be a doctor. I believe that doctors' notes are messy because they have to write a lot of information very quickly.

When I was last at the dentist, I saw him make a note that he had explained to me that drilling my pearly whites to fill a cavity might cause my tooth to crack, in which case I might need a root canal. (Do you think he makes such notes with all clients, or do you think it has something to do with my being a litigation lawyer?) My dentist understood the importance of managing client expectations and reducing his risk. With that note in my chart, he would win the credibility battle if I asserted that no such risk was ever explained and that I would not have had the cavity filled if I thought it was risky. Notes remind the professional that indeed they did alert clients to the risks. Without such a note, and in the face of a client who asserted otherwise, the professional— doctor, lawyer, or dentist—could not be certain of having warned the client of the risks. Professional advisors tend to advise many clients each day, without taking notes. Without those notes, however, they cannot specifically recall what transpired with a particular client on a particular day. Advisors who say they do specifically recall events from months or sometimes years before the evidence is given will put their own credibility into question. An experienced lawyer could easily trip up such an advisor during a session of cross-examination.

While advisors complain that taking notes can be arduous, I ask, what side of that credibility battle do advisors want to be on?

III. ADVISORS HELP THEMSELVES BY HELPING THEIR LAWYERS

When examining a judge's or arbitrator's reasons for a decision, it is useful to ask the following questions:

- Why did the judge believe one party over the other—was it the credibility of the witnesses?

- What helped the winning party convince the judge that his story was more credible?
- Did the witnesses have documentation to support their own version of events?
- What could the advisor have said or done to convince the judge to believe his story?
- For those decisions that find in favor of the advisor, what evidence did the judge find compelling?

In the next section of this chapter, specific cases will be examined to determine why certain testimony was preferred. We will look at why conducting business in a manner that can render an advisor's testimony more credible may also increase client satisfaction and decrease the likelihood of complaints—the proverbial killing of two birds with one stone.

CASE #1: CREDIBILITY VICTORY

You've likely heard many stories of advisors who failed to know their client and suffered the wrath of judges and arbitrators. Do judges and arbitrators ever believe advisors? They do. In this 2002 decision by a regulator,[3] the client, Mr. G, claimed that his advisor, Shanks, failed to learn the essential facts about him, that his recommendations were unsuitable, that accounts were churned, and that he engaged in discretionary trading.

Mr. G's net worth was about $1.25 million. Shanks opened a margin account for his client. Shanks completed his firm's new client application form, but the form did not contain specific requirements to attribute the percentage breakdown to either the risk factors or investment objectives.

Mr. G said he didn't understand how a margin account operated nor had he ever expressed any desire to speculate. He also testified that Shanks must have engaged in discretionary trading, because he had not given the advisor any instructions. Shanks testified that he recalled several discussions with his client and that Mr. G understood margin accounts. To prove this, he produced a spreadsheet Mr. G

---

3. *Gregory Pepper Shanks* (2002), IDA Bulletin 3028 (Alberta District Council).

had prepared and given to him. This document served as evidence of Mr. G's sophistication and understanding. Under cross-examination, Mr. G admitted he had previously engaged in speculative investing. He also admitted that he remembered some of the conversations Shanks had described in his testimony.

Though the new client application form was lacking, the District Council concluded that Shanks had not violated his obligation to learn the essential facts about his client. The KYC form "is just the beginning of the know your client obligation"[4] and does not constitute everything embraced in this term. There is the knowledge that the broker gains as he becomes familiar with his customer and the latter's dealings in the market. Accordingly, the decision was based on what the advisor knew about the client, beyond the form.

Though the investments in the margin account were speculative, the suitability of the investments was linked to Mr. G's sophistication. Although the client said he was unsophisticated, the advisor's testimony that he was sophisticated was believed due to the documentation prepared by Mr. G that Shanks kept in his file. Shanks could recall details of conversations he had with the client, including particulars of Mr. G's experience. Furthermore, Mr. G's other speculative investments rendered his evidence less believable. The District Council decided in the advisor's favor, concluding that the investments were suitable.

On the issue of churning, which was also alleged, the District Council concluded that to prove churning, the following elements had to be present: excessive trading, the advisor exercising control over the trading, like in a discretionary account; and the advisor having an ulterior motive, for example, earning excessive commissions. Based on the client's evidence, those elements were absent.

Mr. G's inconsistencies and failure to recollect details led the District Council to favor the advisor's version of events. As a result, the advisor maintained his reputation and his license— and he returned his checkbook to his drawer.

That is the happy ending to this credibility story.

---

4.   ibid. at page 2

Advisors may think that the issue of credibility in court does not affect them because they don't ever expect to be witnesses in court. But beware: with the increased number of client claims and complaints, it may not be a question of *if* but of **when** an advisor will be sued or called onto the regulator's carpet.

Good record-keeping habits can improve an advisor's credibility in court and get advisors into the habit of complying with regulatory and legal obligations.

CASE #2: CREDIBILITY PROBLEM

Let's look at another case.[5] Mr. H was an engineer in his 50s when he met Mr. B, his broker. Mr. H had previously invested heavily in stocks and options, but he did not have much money.

Mr. B was an experienced advisor with the chartered accountant designation. He specialized in option investments and developed a special strategy for index options. On Mr. B's advice, Mr. H's account consisted mostly of uncovered options—speculative and highly leveraged. Mr. H began to lose money and had to sell stock to cover a margin call. He decided to sell his entire account because he could not afford to lose any more money and instructed Mr. B accordingly. Mr. B encouraged Mr. H to hold onto the account. He did so but suffered further losses.

The dealer, through which Mr. B was licensed, sued the client for over $250,000—the amount owing in his margin account after it was closed out. Mr. H counterclaimed against the dealer, asserting failure to supervise, and against Mr. B, asserting that he breached his duty by recommending unsuitable investments and by refusing to follow Mr. H's instructions to sell.

Both the client and advisor were witnesses. In the reasons for his decision, the judge described the advisor as follows, "He carries with him an air of knowledge, competence and assurance." The judge's description of the client was as follows, "He struck me as a sincere, soft spoken person, not aggressive or combative.

---

5.   *Nesbitt Thomson Deacon Inc. v. Haupt* [1992] O.J. No. 552 (O.C.J. Gen. Div.) (QL).

While he appeared knowledgeable about the stock market he also appeared somewhat naively optimistic."[6]

The judge described the advisor-client relationship as that of teacher and student. ". . . [The advisor] was the guru in this very specialized field and I concluded that . . . [the client] placed his trust and reliance in him almost totally."[7]

The judge ruled in favor of the client, concluding that the "naively optimistic" client trusted his advisor.

But there is more to this matter than meets the eye. The outcome of this case may have been different if the advisor had responded properly to several red flags. There was little evidence that the advisor listened to and followed the client's instructions. Advisors need to follow their clients' instructions and document that they have done so. If the advisor had followed the client's instructions and had letters or notes to reflect the communication, he may not have received the complaint in the first place. No doubt, the advisor lost the client and suffered bad publicity, as did the dealer.

CASE #3: CREDIBILITY DISASTER

Insurance professionals struggle to identify potential sources of risk arising from a complicated chain of individuals intertwined in a web that even the brightest legal minds struggle to untangle. This web, referred to as "agency and principal," is well illustrated in the following decision.[8] Although this case is a property and casualty insurance case, its principles apply to any advisor in the securities and insurance industry.

Audio Works, an audio equipment rental business, retained a firm of insurance agents to procure coverage. The agents, in turn, approached an insurer's broker liaison and requested liability and property insurance coverage on terms that included in-transit and replacement coverage. The broker obtained coverage from the insurer for the plaintiff on substantially different terms;

6.   ibid. at p.3
7.   ibid. at p.3
8.   *Audio Works Production Services Ltd. v. Canadian Northern Shield Insurance Company et al.,* 2005 MBQB 209 (Q.B.)

specifically, the policy did not provide in-transit coverage or replacement cost coverage.

What can go wrong, will go wrong—a highway accident resulted in substantial damage to transported audio equipment. The insurer denied coverage because the policy did not include in-transit coverage. The insurance agents, the insurer, the managing general agent and its employee, and the broker liaison were involved in a six-year lawsuit for the replacement cost of the damaged audio equipment.

The trial judge decided in Audio Works' favor and ordered reimbursement. The presiding judge pointed to the lack of documentation to support the broker's testimony. The broker testified that he specifically told the client that his policy excluded "in-transit" coverage; the broker didn't have any notes, letters, memos, or e-mails. Accordingly, the judge decided in favor of Audio Works, ordering reimbursement. The judge reviewed the written insurance application that specifically requested in-transit coverage and found that this documentation was evidence of what the applicant requested. Unless there was documentation specifically explaining the material differences between the application for insurance and the ultimate policy, the applicant should be permitted to rely on the application.

The lesson is that paper trails win cases. A judge is far more likely to accept the version of events supported by complete, accurate notes, correspondence, and documentation. In particular, notes of all meetings and telephone conversations should be in the client file, and all agreements should be in writing and confirmed by the relevant parties. The judge is likely to accept the version of events that is supported by a systematically prepared paper trail.

Finally, judges will submit insurance agents, brokers, and MGAs to the same standards of competence expected from other professionals.

The Audio Works' litigation cost each party in the chain a hefty sum, not to mention aggravation and bad publicity. If there was evidence, other than perhaps small print on a policy, that the client had been informed of the limitations to coverage, the lawsuit may have been avoided.

Different parties along the insurance industry chain work together to sell insurance products that limit a client's risk. Each of these parties is affected individually when clients sue; each must hire legal counsel to defend their respective positions; and each takes a personal or corporate hit to their reputation. Learning to manage risks can lead to better results for the insurance company, MGA, advisor, and, ultimately, the client, who should understand the limits to his insurance coverage.

All advisors benefit from keeping a record of events. Whether handwritten, electronic, or otherwise, notes assist advisors to remember what transpired and give them confidence that their version of events is more accurate than the client's. In court or before a regulator, evidence that supports the advisor's version of events will enable the advisor to be more convincing. The client's version, not supported by any record, will be dismissed, as will the client's claim.

IV. WINNING THE CREDIBILITY BATTLE

The balance of this chapter explores methods to employ to win the credibility battle against clients in court and in regulatory proceedings.

THE IMPORTANCE OF A CONTEMPORANEOUS RECORD

Regardless of the type of record kept, it is crucial that a record be maintained that was prepared contemporaneously with the events. This simply means that the record is made at the time of the meeting or telephone conversation with the client. Some advisors prepare few or no records during the meetings and telephone calls but much later may insert a note, completed without any supporting details, into the file or forms. Such a record is not evidence of what was said during the meeting, but rather is evidence of the advisor's *best recollection* of what was discussed. Judges and arbitrators do not find notes taken after the fact to be as reliable as notes taken during the meeting.

TYPES OF RECORDS:

Handwritten Notes

Many advisors complain that their handwriting is illegible and throw up their hands insisting that they cannot write down everything that is said. Perfection, however, is not the standard. Years later, even the most cryptic notes help advisors remember what was discussed. Poorly prepared handwritten notes are far better than no notes at all.

My handwriting is horrible. However, as messy as my notes are, they are written for each and every telephone call that I have with clients. I use a form that has a space for the date and time at the top, a space for the name of the person with whom I spoke, and a space for any action items that my assistant and I need to follow up on. Advisors can design forms to meet their own needs or see the template of the form I use. I also choose colored paper, so that these notes stand out from other written correspondence (letters or e-mails) delivered to clients. My notes and correspondence are organized on a metal spike in reverse chronological order, and placed in a yellow folder. Here are some additional suggestions for advisors preparing handwritten notes:

- Put the date and time at the beginning of the notes, and put the time again at the bottom.
- Make a horizontal line at the bottom of the page to indicate the end of the notes.
- Indicate in the notes the names of individuals at the meeting or on the telephone call.
- Put any follow-up items at the end of the notes.

SAMPLE TELEPHONE SHEET

TELEPHONE CALL

Re: _____

By: Ellen Bessner

File Number: _____

TO: _____

FROM: _____

DATE: 20___ / _____ / _____
                        M   D

☐ Left Message to Call Back
☐ Left Voice-Mail Message

TIME: _____

ACTION REQUIRED:

_____

_____

_____

_____

_____

_____

_____

_____

_____

_____

_____

TIME: _____

Typed Notes

Because my writing is so slow and illegible, and my typing is quite good, I take my laptop to important meetings. As these notes are typed instead of handwritten, they don't need to be transcribed. After my notes are spell-checked and printed, they are filed away until they are needed.

In the financial and insurance industries, where business is conducted quickly after several telephone calls and meetings, software programs exist that simplify the recording of conversations by automatically inserting date and time. These programs permit several advisors and their assistants to insert notes and then print out a summary of conversations in chronological order. This allows each member of a team to better service clients as they can ascertain what was previously discussed with the client, without having to first track down an advisor who may or may not be in the office when the client calls. The efficiency of such a system depends on the quality and quantity of notes inserted. I have heard that assistants find the advisors' notes are often missing or too cryptic. If advisors and dealers spend money on the software, they should use it.

Some systems of storage and retrieval render the above method more efficient and less expensive. Advisors must know how to store and retrieve the notes that were taken on a computer, as the printouts of these electronic notes are invaluable if, years later, advisors and dealers are challenged by clients.

Letters or e-mails

Instead of writing time-consuming letters, some advisors send newsletters in an effort to differentiate themselves from their competitors.

While newsletters are fine, a letter or e-mail specific to the client's circumstances is often necessary. For example, if the advisor questions whether the client fully understood a conversation they had in person or over the telephone, it might be wise to clarify the exchange in writing. A letter or e-mail from the advisor clarifying the matter of concern is very powerful in court or at the regulator, particularly if it exudes professionalism and is received by the client either before he makes a decision based on the advisor's recommendations or before he suffers significant losses.

To ensure that the letter or e-mail clearly sets out the advisor's concern and reflects his or her professionalism without making damaging admissions, I recommend that advisors show their letters or e-mails to the compliance department before sending them. This kind of correspondence is a great way to avoid client complaints about advisors and/or dealers and at least supports the advisor's version of events if a complaint arises. When advisors work with clients who continually push the envelope, it is a good idea to consistently send letters and e-mails to the client, throughout the relationship.

Taping

I remember many years ago, I was speaking at a conference and someone raised his hand and asked me whether he should tape-record client meetings. I told him as long as the client was aware and agreeable, it was fine. But I couldn't envisage a client being that comfortable or agreeable. However, another gentle-looking man raised his hand and told me that he taped all client meetings, and he didn't encounter reluctance from clients because he reassured them about taping meetings. He told clients he taped because what was discussed was very important to him, and he concentrates better if he does not have to take notes. If clients are sufficiently comfortable with taping, it is an efficient way to record details of what the client has told the advisor. The gentleman at the meeting suggested that once clients get used to meetings being taped, they usually expect a tape recorder at all future meetings. However, if clients seem inhibited or uncomfortable with tape recorders, they may hold back information. For them, this method would be ineffective.

If the dealer or advisor chooses to tape meetings, a system of storing and retrieving the tapes is absolutely necessary. Advisors need to check applicable laws in their jurisdiction, which may prohibit taping or which may require obtaining client consent or taking other steps before turning on the tape recorder. Local privacy laws will likely prohibit advisors and dealers from using the tapes for purposes other than furthering the advisor-client relationship or defending themselves if sued by the client.

Advisors should keep in mind that tape recorders can, and often do, malfunction. When taping, it's a good idea to use more than one tape recorder as backup and/or to write notes simultaneously. Before a meeting, it is essential to check that batteries work. It is also smart to have extra batteries and/or an electrical outlet nearby. As for transcribing a tape, this should be done as soon as possible. The longer one waits, the harder it can be to decipher all the words on the tape.

Telephone Conversations

Many advisors have asked me whether they should tape all communication, particularly telephone conversations with clients. Setting aside my concern about the volume of tapes and the ability to store and retrieve them, my concern is that advisors will forget the tape is running. The result might be sloppy language. If tapes are maintained and if a client sues, the client's lawyer would be entitled to have a copy of the tapes. This is also the case if the regulator asks for the tapes. In most jurisdictions, regulators are entitled to have them, regardless of whether they hurt or help the advisor. I have listened to several taped conversations between advisors and their clients and, if I can generalize, these tapes may bolster the client's case and, at best, are neutral for the advisor's case. Unless advisors can install a mechanism that makes them constantly aware that the tape recorder is running, I cannot recommend this practice. I think it would be almost impossible to always remember that the tape is on and to ensure that advisors watch their "P's" and "Q's" during every conversation, with every client, every day. Some advisors use the following technique: they imagine that a regulatory compliance person listens to all conversations between advisors and clients and is always judging their professionalism. This helps them to remember the tape is running.

V.   MARKING TRADES UNSOLICITED[9]

Advisors should help their lawyers and themselves by properly marking trades "unsolicited" and having paper trails to prove that

---

9.   These are general comments on this subject. For more detail, check the regulations in your jurisdiction or check with your branch manager or compliance officer.

trades were unsolicited. Earlier in the book, we discussed this topic in the context of suitability and clients pushing the advisor to over-concentrate the account. Now, we will explore what constitutes an unsolicited trade.

An unsolicited trade is when the client initiates a purchase or sale of a particular security in his or her account. It does not matter who placed the initial phone call or asked for the meeting. What matters is who initiated the particular transaction.

When a client initiates a purchase of a security with which the advisor is unfamiliar, the advisor has the following choices, assuming she understands the product sufficiently for suitability purposes:

- She can advise the client that she does not follow the security and can buy it for the client and mark it unsolicited. The client, however, will have to follow the security to ascertain when to sell it.
- She can buy it for the client account, follow it, and advise the client when to sell. In this scenario, the purchase may be unsolicited, but the sale will be solicited.
- She can ask the client to buy it in his self-directed discount account because she does not follow it.

Regardless which route (these or others) the advisor takes, notes must exist to back up the conversation. A confirming letter to the client will bolster the advisor's position.

What if the security is unsuitable? The advisor should examine whether the client's risk tolerance has changed and, as explained more fully in Chapter 4, what precipitated the change. If no evidence exists to support such a change, the advisor should refuse to purchase the product. She could tell the client that if he is committed to trading in this security, he could open a discount account. In such a case, however, there would be a note in the file that the advisor cautioned the client against making the purchase.

SUB-FILES TO MAINTAIN ORDER IN CLIENT FILES

The following sub-files are suggested to maintain the client materials:

- all correspondence between the client and the advisor;
- all notes taken at every meeting and during telephone conversations with the client;
- all advertising and marketing material delivered to the client by e-mail or in other ways;
- all signed documents, including the KYC form, insurance applications, and investment policy statements;
- all documents that include notes of discussions describing a leverage loan and the risk associated with it, and all sign-off materials (leverage loan disclosure statements) pertaining to a client who has taken a leverage loan; and
- evidence of delivery of important documents (including insurance applications to insurance companies) and important letters to clients.

SUMMARY

Credibility can win the day. Appreciating the importance of credibility in court and in regulatory matters is the first step to winning the credibility battle. Advisors who use the techniques discussed in this chapter will be better equipped to win the credibility war and, ultimately, to get favorable results if a complaint is lodged. The alternative should not be an option. Using the defensive strategies outlined will mitigate losses for advisors and dealers, and will boost the advisor's professionalism.

ADVISORS TAKE ACTION

✓ Question your clients and document the answers to understand and obtain evidence of their levels of sophistication.

✓ Maintain a record and paper trail of all communications that occur between you and the client.

✓ Take or record notes every time you talk to clients on the phone or in a meeting. Whether the notes are handwritten, electronic, or transcribed from a tape, they should be complete, accurate, and contemporaneous.

✓ Write letters or e-mails, particularly to clarify a specific issue or item discussed earlier.

✓ When you mark trades unsolicited, ensure you have documentation to corroborate that it was indeed an unsolicited trade.

CHAPTER 7
Manage Your Clients

To enjoy a successful career, advisors need clients who respect their professionalism and integrity, and who understand that advisors must adhere to a set of rules to maintain their license. Most clients fit this description. In my career defending advisors, however, I have met a disproportionate number of advisors' clients who do not understand and, in some cases, who do not respect their advisor's professionalism and integrity. While advisors have been in the spotlight, accused of being "Rogue Brokers," in some cases it is "Rogue Clients" who may be the source of problems for advisors.

Advisors often express a sincere liking for their clients. They may, however, have one problematic client out of a large client base. Problem clients can be young or old, close friends, family members, or strangers. The following kinds of people can be problem clients:

- someone who is simply uncooperative or too demanding to allow the advisor to conduct business in a compliant way;
- someone who is deliberately evasive and doesn't provide the advisor with adequate information, so that he can later blame the advisor for investments with negative consequences; and
- someone who actually attempts to use the advisor to carry out illegal or extremely high-risk activity that will only end in increased expense, effort, and liability for the advisor.

These problem clients can manipulate situations, so that they benefit whether or not their account increases. That's because they are regularly reimbursed by the trail of advisors and dealers they leave behind.

Although it is important to maintain a clear paper trail for every client, special attention must be paid to documenting all communication with these types of clients, because these clients may have no difficulty changing their stories. If advisors do not document conversations with these clients, advisors will be at their mercy in court or at the regulatory hearing.

I. IDENTIFYING "PROBLEM" CLIENTS

PASSIVE-AGGRESSIVE CLIENTS

Some clients may seem passive in their relationships with their advisors, but they may be prepared to launch a complaint if their account suffers losses. They might encourage the advisor to take risks, but they also expect the advisor to take full responsibility for any losses. They may be polite when they hear from their advisor and seem to listen to advice. But they instruct their advisor according to what they want to buy, regardless of their advisor's recommendations. When they lose money, these are the first clients to assert that they didn't understand the risks or that the investments were unsuitable. These clients may be particularly dangerous because they can be manipulative and give their advisors a false sense of comfort: advisors tend to believe that these clients will never complain.

SUPER-AGGRESSIVE CLIENTS

These clients are somewhat more transparent than passive-aggressive types, as they tend to push advisors hard and ignore their advice. While we want clients to be engaged in their investment choices, clients who are aggressive with their advisors may be dangerous if advisors allow these clients to push them to ignore their regulatory or legal obligations. This can occur when an account needs to be rebalanced because it is too heavily weighted in a single security or sector that has increased in value. The advisor calls the client and explains the need to rebalance, noting that the stock price could fall and the client could lose money. But the client refuses to sell a portion of the investment to rebalance his or her holdings. This places the advisor in a terrible position.

While no law compels clients to sell their winners, there are laws and regulations that require advisors to maintain balanced, rather than over-concentrated, accounts for their clients. However, advisors cannot sell without their clients' instructions. Yet if the particular sector or investment diminishes in value, the client may not hesitate to look to the advisor for reimbursement, threatening to complain to the regulator.

There have been court cases in which the advisor was held responsible for losses even though the client was knowledgeable and experienced. Why? Because courts have held that although the client was knowledgeable, the advisor could have better explained the risks and documented that sufficient warning was provided. Advisors must beware of the risks they may take at the insistence of aggressive clients. They must manage such clients by explaining their legal and regulatory obligations and by insisting that such obligations be followed—otherwise, the advisor can expect to write a big check one day.

COMPLAINERS

These are clients who complain about the service, the returns, the commissions, the complexity of the statements, the frequency or infrequency of the statements, and anything and everything that relates to their investments or insurance products. There are clients who complain about everything. They complain when investments diminish in value and, when investments rise in value, they complain that they didn't rise enough.

Of course, there is a big difference between groundless whining and legitimate feedback. Listening to the complaints and considering the legitimacy of each complaint is important. In the service industry, we should value clients who express legitimate concerns, and we should manage or fire clients who constantly complain and are ungrateful for our hard work.

Advisors need to be wary of clients who complain about everything because this is a sign that they do not appreciate how hard professionals work to satisfy them. If they don't get the results they want—and their expectations are often unreasonable—off to the regulator or the courts they go.

ABUSIVE CLIENTS

Money can be an emotional topic for clients and, when they lose money, they can react badly. To some degree, this is understandable. However, certain clients are downright abusive. They believe they get better service this way. Their abuses can be limitless and may include yelling, threats, or spreading rumors about the advisor. Some advisors refuse to service these types of clients; others accept the abuse because they are trying to build their book of business. By accepting the client, they also accept the risk involved. It is quite a risk because clients who throw their weight around with their advisors do not hesitate to throw it around in the form of regulatory complaints or litigation.

PACIFISTS

These clients give advisors their money and tell them that their job is to make them more money, but not to bother them. They may have busy careers or other obligations. They refuse to listen to explanations of the risks or the nature of the investments and don't want to give their advisors specific instructions. These clients commonly tell the advisor, "Don't call me. Just sell and buy when you think you should." An advisor who succumbs to these wishes engages in discretionary trading in his clients' accounts. Unless an advisor is licensed to manage portfolios on a discretionary basis, he is committing a serious regulatory infraction that could cost him his license.

DECEPTIVE / UNTRUTHFUL CLIENTS

A minority of clients lie to their advisors. These clients are the veritable rogues. They are dishonest concerning their personal assets or liabilities. Perhaps they hide assets due to mistrust. Perhaps they fear their advisor will try to sell them additional insurance or attempt to obtain more of their net worth if they tell the truth about their assets. Perhaps they fear that if they tell the advisor the truth about their financial situation, it will not be kept completely confidential from the tax authorities or from the spouse from whom they recently separated. Whatever the motivation, such deception is dangerous for advisors. They cannot fulfill their basic know-your-client and other regulatory and legal obligations without the truth about the client's assets, liabilities, and financial obligations.

Arguably, these clients are the most dangerous. They are comfortable deceiving people and may lie about anything. I firmly believe that in any relationship, trust is a two-way street, and I find it most disturbing that the emphasis is only on advisors needing to be trustworthy. What about clients? Advisors have a right to insist that their clients are honest and open because business is based on a foundation of trust that goes both ways.

FRIENDS AND FAMILY

Though friends and family are often a great source of referrals, advisors must be cautious when mixing friends and family with business because advisors tend to let their guard down, mistakenly believing that these trusted clients will never launch a complaint against them. In fact, some of these relationships display a dark side—especially if the client loses money.

Advisors may be prepared to break the rules to benefit these clients and are lulled into a false sense of security because they believe that close friends and family would never blow the whistle. For example, the advisor may allow friends and family to over-concentrate their accounts or invest in unsuitable investments. But if the clients lose money, advisors may be surprised to find their close friends or relatives launching proceedings, saying, "It's only business."

The well-publicized Canadian case *R. v. Andrew Rankin*[1] exemplifies this risk. Andrew Rankin's childhood friend Daniel Duic sold him down the river. Rankin was an investment banker who is alleged to have shared confidential information with Duic after being, in the words of the trial judge, "pestered, prodded, pleaded and plied with alcohol, extracting confidential information concerning investment deals." Duic purchased and sold investments based upon this confidential information. When Rankin learned that the regulator was on their trail, he promptly contacted Duic to let him know. Duic immediately moved substantial proceeds to an offshore bank and contacted the regulator to cut a deal that would save his hide but sink his friend. In exchange for not being pursued by the regulator, Duic agreed to testify against Rankin. Amazingly enough, the regulator permitted Duic to keep a substantial amount of his investment

---

1.　*R. v. Rankin*, [2006] O.J. No. 4579, (Prov. Ct.), rev'd [2007] O.J. No. 719 (C.A.).

proceeds. Rankin was criminally charged with tipping and insider trading. The trial judge found him guilty on several counts of tipping and sentenced him to six months in prison, which was successfully appealed and a new trial ordered.[2] Although the trial judge had nothing nice to say about Duic, this did Rankin little good.

Advisors may believe that if the regulatory panel or judge perceives the client to be a rogue, the advisor will appear less so and is more likely to avoid an order. Advisors may also think that in such circumstances, the penalties or damages they receive will be significantly reduced. This is not the case. Although a judge or regulatory panel may not sympathize with a rogue client, advisors will not be off the hook if they have breached their regulatory or legal obligations.

What should advisors do if they identify a rogue client and, after several attempts to work matters through, cannot meet the client's unreasonable expectations? My advice: if you cannot manage them, face the music before it faces you!

II. WHAT IF THE CLIENT'S EXPECTATIONS ARE UNREASONABLE?

ADVISORS SHOULD NOT BE OSTRICHES

If a client's expectations are unreasonable and all effort to communicate with the client has failed, advisors should not hide from the client. Instead, they need to deal with the matter head on. If the client won't change, the advisor must fire the client.

WEED OUT UNREASONABLE CLIENTS

To be a professional advisor, one needs to rise above clients who expect the impossible. This means identifying such clients early on and taking a professional approach to weeding them out. Needless to say, through the weeding-out process, advisors will need to liaise with their branch managers and/or compliance officers.

---

2. In February 2008, Andrew Rankin and the Ontario Securities Commission entered into a settlement whereby all charges were withdrawn in exchange for the following: an admission by Andrew Rankin that he engaged in illegal tipping, a payment toward the OSC's costs of $250,000, a lifetime ban from working in the securities industry or serving as a director or officer of a public company, and a 10-year ban on trading securities in Ontario.

FIRE CLIENTS

Can an advisor fire a client? Absolutely, but there is a right and a wrong way to do it. First, with the help of compliance officers or the dealer's legal staff, the advisor should examine the written provisions of any contractual agreement to determine how each party can terminate the relationship. Most commercial contracts state that the terminating party must advise the other party of the intention to terminate the contract before the actual termination. This provision may specify how the message of the intention to terminate must be delivered; for example: "10-days advance written notice to be delivered by registered mail to the following address: …" However, the written terms of agreement between an advisor and a client do not usually contemplate termination. In fact, if the advisor sells insurance products, then the written agreement is not between the advisor and the client but between the client and the insurance company. Instead, the advisor can refuse to work with the client in the future. Advisors need to be particularly careful, however, to confirm all terminations in writing, particularly if renewals are an issue.

When terminating an agreement, advisors must give clients reasonable notice in the particular circumstances. The issue of dependency is also significant in determining whether the loss of the benefit of the contract would severely impact the party being terminated. This legal principle is well established in commercial contracts.[3] For example, consider an exclusive contract for S (supplier) to supply widgets to P (purchaser) for a price. If the contract has been in place for several years, and S has purchased inventory assuming P will continue to buy S's widgets, and if P is S's only customer, then P will be required to provide S with notice of termination for a period longer than if S had only been providing P with widgets for a few months and also supplies several other customers. In this example, S has become reliant upon the financial benefits of the relationship with P, and P will be obliged to provide a longer period of notice before being able to terminate the contract with S.

---

3.   *Hillis Oil & Sales Ltd. v. Wynn's Canada Ltd.* [1986] S.C.R. 57.

Advisors should ask themselves the following questions to determine what a reasonable notice period would be for clients whom they intend to terminate:

Is the client dependent on the advisor?

Among other issues, the sophistication, age, and health of the client, and the complexity of the investments are important elements to review in determining whether or not the client may be perceived to be dependent on the advisor. The more dependent the client is on the advisor, the longer the period of notice that may be required.

Another factor is whether the client resides in a location in which there are several advisors. For example, competent advisors abound in large North American cities. However, if the client resides in a small town with few advisors, it would be reasonable to expect it would take the client more time to replace the advisor. The client may need to travel to a different town.

Is the timing of the termination prejudicial to the client?

Timing is everything. Professionals cannot terminate their relationships with clients when it might be detrimental or prejudicial to the client. In most circumstances, lawyers cannot terminate their relationships with clients on the day before a big court hearing. The lawyer will likely be compelled to continue to represent the client to avoid any prejudice. Likewise, the advisor cannot abandon the client just minutes before steps must be taken, without which the client will be detrimentally affected. For example, an investment advisor (licensed to sell most types of securities) cannot terminate the relationship with the client when the client instructs the advisor to sell the investment that is falling like a rock. If the advisor refuses the suitable trade on the basis that he has at that moment, without prior notice, advised the client that the relationship is terminated, the advisor may be held responsible for any losses the client suffers as a result. It is better to terminate the relationship well in advance of any client order or investment coming due, so that the client can arrange to transfer the investment account.

Make peace with the client first.

It is better to terminate the relationship when there is peace. If the relationship ends in anger, it is more likely that the advisor will be sued or a complaint will be made to the regulator.

How should notice of termination be communicated?

I recommend an oral explanation that does not insult the client and that is gently and professionally relayed. An insulted client is more likely to complain to the regulator or commence litigation. A bit of sensitivity may go a long way. An accountant once told me of his decision to drop several clients at once, doing so before tax season. The accountant had built areas of his practice that he found far more interesting than tax returns, and he could afford to part from his tax clients. Time consuming though it was, he called each of the clients personally, left messages for those whom he didn't speak to, and followed up with a polite letter several months before tax-return time.

There is no reason why an advisor cannot terminate relationships with clients. The important thing is to ensure that it is done in a manner that reduces, rather than increases, the advisor's risks. The advisor should carefully plan the termination by choosing its manner and timing and by giving the client sufficient notice at a time that isn't prejudicial to the client. That way the client has time to locate and hire a new advisor.

SUMMARY

Unfortunately, some of an advisor's clients can create more problems in the long term than their short-term business justifies. It is probably a good idea to routinely try to identify those troublesome relationships early on and to end them sooner rather than later. To do so makes an advisor more efficient.

ADVISORS TAKE ACTION

✓ Although there may be few problem clients, it is important to identify them.

✓ Passive-aggressive clients: It is especially important to maintain a clear paper trail with this type of client.

✓ Super-aggressive clients: These might be the most obvious problem clients to spot, and also the most unpleasant. Advisors are professionals and should not accept such treatment.

✓ Complainers: Listen to and consider the legitimacy of all of their complaints. Be wary of clients who complain about everything.

✓ Abusive clients: Some advisors refuse to deal with them; other advisors accept the abuse because of the potential payout. In making your decision, remember these clients may also be prepared to make complaints and start litigation.

✓ Pacifists: Making discretionary trades for client accounts without being licensed to do so is a serious regulatory infraction.

✓ Deceptive/Untruthful clients: Offering advice based on outdated or incorrect information can be dangerous because advisors cannot fulfill their regulatory know-your-client obligations.

✓ Friends and family: Don't be lulled into a false sense of security. Even your best friend can betray you.

✓ Ascertain whether your clients' expectations are reasonable. If their expectations are unreasonable, terminate these clients, ensuring that you do so at a time that does not adversely impact them.

CHAPTER 8
Invisible Clients

Mr. Roses is a client who is just months away from his 98th birthday. He was healthy until last month when he was admitted to hospital with a minor stroke. Mr. Roses has had the same advisor for many years. Noel, his son and power of attorney—and likely the beneficiary of his estate—also has a sizable account with his father's advisor. Noel has been pleased with the returns on his own account. However, his father has very conservative investments and, for the past couple of years, has only earned an average of 5% on his investments. The market is strong and Noel tells his advisor that he wants to change the investments in his father's account, making them riskier. Noel says his father will be better off if the account is more aligned with his own, pointing out that his returns are higher than his father's.

To maintain good relations with Noel, the advisor may be tempted to follow his instructions. She could change the KYC documentation. If she does, and if it is not caught by her supervisor or a compliance officer, a legitimate claim may be launched against her and her dealer if the account loses money. A better scenario would be if a conscientious branch manager or compliance officer refuses to sign off on the new KYC form and instead asks why a 98-year-old is substantially increasing his risk tolerance.

The example cited above is particularly relevant because as the client population ages, baby boomers take more control over their elderly parents' accounts. The above issue also has relevance in spousal situations.

Mr. and Mrs. Stevens have been married for 14 years. Michael Stevens has had an advisor for years and has instructed the advisor about his wife's account, too. The advisor has never met Michael's wife, Effany Stevens, but has a KYC form for her, which he completed according to Michael's instructions. Michael indicated that Effany's risk tolerance is medium high, like his own. In fact, the couple's KYC forms are almost identical. Michael does not have a joint account with Effany, but he has power of attorney on each of her accounts. He deposits and withdraws, while Effany is not at all involved in her own accounts. She signs whatever her husband brings home for her to sign. In fact, Effany is not interested in these financial issues. Her energies are primarily focused on their three children, her full-time job, and the care and maintenance of their household. For his part, Michael works long hours operating his retail store, which finances their comfortable lifestyle.

I.   WHO IS AN INVISIBLE CLIENT?

This is a client who is invisible to the advisor either because he or she chooses to be or because a person with power of attorney instructs the advisor on behalf of the client. When thinking it through, the advisor who dons his "protect myself" hat as opposed to his "grow-my-book-of-business" hat might realize that the client is invisible. The advisor might then try to ensure that he fulfills his obligations to that client by first asking himself the following questions:

- For this account and in these circumstances, who is my client?
- Am I operating the account in a manner that is in the client's best interest?
- Is the KYC form in keeping with the client's risk tolerance and personal objectives, or is it instead in keeping with the risk tolerance and personal objectives of the person instructing me on the account?
- If the client knew of the risks associated with the investments in her account, would she be comfortable?
- If the client was engaged in the investment process, would she agree with the instructions of her power of attorney?
- What powers and limits to these powers are evident in the power of attorney document signed by the client?
- If there was a regulatory audit of this account, would it pass the regulator's scrutiny?
- If the account diminishes in value, could the client or her beneficiaries succeed in a claim against me for damages?

- How do I explain to a long-time client that I have decided I need to change the risk tolerance? How do I do this without losing my client and her account?

II. POWERS OF ATTORNEY AND INVISIBLE CLIENTS

While people with powers of attorney may be well-intentioned, they may not appreciate the obligations that advisors have to their clients. Advisors have both regulatory and legal obligations to always act in their clients' best interests. The advisor should think through every issue associated with any change or trade and, if unsure, discuss with the branch manager or compliance staff whether the trade is being made for reasons other than the benefit of the true client.

Advisors should read the power of attorney document carefully. Each document is different, and advisors must familiarize themselves with the rights and obligations inherent in the particular power of attorney signed by the advisor's client. If an advisor's firm uses a particular form, advisors must familiarize themselves with that form.

Remember what a power of attorney is: if advisors read the document carefully, they will see that it likely **permits**, rather than compels, the advisor to take instructions from the person or people named as the power of attorney. What does that mean? If clients like Mrs. Stevens can provide the advisor with instructions, then the advisor is not compelled to take instructions from her power of attorney, Mr. Stevens. The advisor has every right and, in certain circumstances, an obligation to check the instructions with the person who is actually the client.

Advisors tend to confuse the person who has the power of attorney with the actual client. The client is the person in whose name the account is held. The client's risk tolerance and objectives are the ones that count and not the risk tolerance and objectives of the person carrying the power of attorney. This can be particularly confusing when the person with power of attorney has his own account with the same advisor. It is even more confusing when the person with power of attorney believes that he is likely to be the beneficiary of the estate. The emphasis is on the word "likely" because a Last Will and Testament can be changed at any time without anyone's knowledge. This means that nobody knows with certainty who the ultimate beneficiary is until a person dies and his or her will is read. Furthermore, other beneficiaries may share the estate.

Keep in mind, while Mr. Roses is in the hospital, he may be fully capable of making decisions for himself. Therefore, if possible, communication should continue with Mr. Roses until it is clear that he no longer wants to instruct his advisor or can no longer do so coherently. But even after Mr. Roses is no longer interested or able to instruct his advisor directly, the advisor must never forget that Mr. Roses, and not his power of attorney, is the client. The advisor needs to ensure that the risk tolerance reflects the client rather than his power of attorney. With respect to any changes to the account, the advisor should err on the side of conservatism.

If Mr. Roses was giving instructions, would he want this changed?

An advisor needs to ask herself whether the instructions given by the person with power of attorney are in Mr. Roses' best interests. The advisor should ask herself whether the change would likely be something Mr. Roses would have instructed her to make, if he was capable of instructing her. If the issue is risk tolerance, the advisor should review the history of the account to determine whether Mr. Roses has ever had a higher risk tolerance. While it is incorrect to state that an elderly person can never have a medium or high risk tolerance, one can assume that a regulator or judge will regard a medium to high risk as unsuitable for a man in his 90s, without some very concrete evidence that this is specifically what he wanted and that he was able to assume such risk.

Are changes consistent with Mr. Roses' Risk Tolerance?

The independent person will ask, "Was this account managed in such a manner that it was consistent with Mr. Roses' risk tolerance, or does it appear to be outside his expected risk tolerance?" If Mr. Roses can instruct the advisor, the advisor should write detailed notes and perhaps a letter of confirmation that explains why the risk tolerance has been adjusted upwards. Without that evidence, the advisor will have great difficulty convincing anyone that the higher risk tolerance reflected Mr. Roses' objectives.

Powers of the Power of Attorney

What powers does the person with power of attorney have to instruct the advisor?[1] This depends upon the details set out in the document.[2] Some dealers do not want to be involved in the choice of the content or the powers granted to the person with power of attorney. Other dealers prefer that their form of power of attorney be the one signed by the client. If the client is of sound mind when this issue arises, the advisor can ask the client to sign the dealer's form.

Whether or not dealers have their own forms, the advisor may want to broach the issue of power of attorney well before a client suffers from poor health. The advisor may want to ask whether the client has signed a power of attorney and, if so, where the document is kept. I suggest discussing this with all clients, regardless of age, either in the context of their parents or in case of an unexpected accident or problem that renders the client unable to instruct the advisor. In most North American jurisdictions, it could be very expensive and time consuming to work out the issue of power of attorney if a client, who has never previously dealt with this issue, becomes incapable of instructing the advisor. Dealing with this issue would likely involve lawyers and court proceedings.[3] If the power of attorney presented to the advisor is not a standard form that the advisor is familiar with, it will need to be read even more carefully. If the advisor does not understand the limits to the powers presented, the advisor will need to ask his branch manager, compliance or legal department for help. Before executing any instructions given by the person with power of attorney, the advisor needs to ensure that the wording of the document of power of attorney permits him to carry out the particular instructions, whether they involve trading, redeeming, or liquidating the account.

The key to managing risk associated with powers of attorney is to understand the documents and to recognize danger signs that

---

1. In most jurisdictions, regulations and internal dealer policies preclude advisors from being appointed as power of attorney for their own clients.
2. The powers granted in powers of attorney are as unique as the person granting them. Powers of attorney may be granted for a broad and vast array of powers.
3. Laws will vary depending upon the jurisdiction.

may signal abuse. While all clients can be vulnerable to people enacting their powers of attorney, invisible clients may be even more vulnerable. That's because the advisor has little or no contact with that person and relies on the person with power of attorney to provide instructions. The advisor anticipates that these instructions are in the best interest of the actual client, but that might not always be the case. An invisible client can be vulnerable to abuses by the person chosen as power of attorney, regardless of who the person is. Here are some examples:

- The client's power of attorney instructs the advisor to place the account in his name, too, making it a joint account.
- After the advisor refuses certain transactions that are not in an elderly client's best interest, the client's power of attorney instructs the advisor to liquidate the account and transfer it to another advisor.
- The client's power of attorney instructs the advisor to invest the money in products that are riskier than what the advisor deems appropriate for the client.
- The client shows signs of memory loss and attends meetings with a son or daughter who, without a power of attorney, instructs the advisor. The client seems to be confused or passive about what is discussed, and decisions are deferred to the son or daughter.

What should the advisor do? Here are some useful steps to take.

Step 1—Advisors should ask themselves the following questions:

- Is there a signed power of attorney?
- Is the client actually incapacitated?
- Do I have a properly signed copy of the document of power of attorney in the client's file?
- What is the date on the power of attorney? Was it signed many years ago? Is it possible that another power of attorney was since signed and I do not have the most recent version?

Assuming the client is of sound mind, like Mrs. Stevens, the advisor should discuss these issues with her. She should understand both the powers conferred by, and the limits to, the document she signed.

If the client is not of sound mind, the advisor will need to discuss his power of attorney with the branch manager or staff in the compliance or legal departments. The advisor cannot assess whether his client has the mental capacity to instruct him, so if there is any doubt in the advisor's mind, he will need to seek help from one of the following people: his branch manager, a compliance officer, or a lawyer.

Step 2—Determine if the client is at risk

Assuming the form conferring rights on the person with power of attorney is properly signed and the advisor understands the limits, the advisor needs to determine whether the instructions from the person with power of attorney place the client at risk. If the client may be at risk, the advisor must immediately notify his or her branch manager and staff in the compliance or legal departments. The advisor would contact these people, for instance, if the person with power of attorney requests a liquidation of all investments, particularly if this would attract deferred sales charges. The advisor would also contact the branch manager and legal and compliance staff if the person with power of attorney asks the advisor to liquidate an account that otherwise operates with decent returns. The advisor should also contact the branch manager, a compliance officer, or in-house lawyer if the person with power of attorney seeks to change the risk tolerance to accept more risk in the client's account. The advisor cannot follow a power of attorney's instructions if they are not in the best interests of the client.

Step 3—Determine that the instructions are in the client's best interest

This issue is more subtle than the issue in Step 2. Instructions from the person with power of attorney could potentially become a problem for the client. For example, it may be true that the client's investments are not increasing at the same rate as those belonging to the person named power of attorney. This may be because the client's risk tolerance is lower than the risk tolerance of the person with power of attorney. Moving the client to a higher risk tolerance may benefit the client if the market performs, but what if the market does not perform? In that case, both the client and the advisor are at risk because the risk tolerance does not reflect the client's real risk tolerance and the investments are, therefore, unsuitable.

III. REGULATORY AND LITIGATION RISKS AND INVISIBLE CLIENTS

REGULATORY RISK

Going back to the example of Mr. Roses, the advisor might ask herself, "If I increase Mr. Roses' risk tolerance, would it pass the scrutiny of a regulatory review?" The regulator can appear for a scheduled or surprise audit. If the regulatory audit includes a review of Mr. Roses' account, which includes medium- to high-risk investments, will the regulator be satisfied that the investments are suitable? Unless there was evidence that explained the change in risk tolerance, the regulatory investigation may be elevated to enforcement proceedings and a penalty.

LITIGATION RISK

What about the risk of litigation? How can one be at risk for litigation when instructions are received from the person who has been appointed power of attorney and who is also the beneficiary of the account? The advisor cannot know with certainty, until after the client passes on and the will is read, who is the beneficiary and whether there is only one beneficiary or several.

As well, an advisor may believe that the person with power of attorney will not sue her because the advisor is following his instructions. Nevertheless, an advisor can never be certain of not being sued. Even if there is only one beneficiary and he is the power of attorney, he could commence litigation against the advisor for losses in the account. If there are several beneficiaries, litigation may be initiated if any unsuitable investments diminished in value. The action may include allegations of breaches of contract and failure to fulfill the duty of a competent advisor. The person suing may thereby claim reimbursement of the capital as well as a reasonable return on the investments. The beneficiaries may also add a claim for punitive damages and, in certain jurisdictions, they may be entitled to obtain reimbursement of their legal costs.

When faced with a situation involving an elderly or incapacitated client, advisors should ask themselves the questions listed above. If such risk analysis makes an advisor break out in hives, it might be wise for the advisor to consult with his branch manager or compliance officers before changing the risk rating of the account. If an advisor does not do so, it may compromise his ethical, legal, and regulatory obligations, as well as his reputation and license.

But how would an advisor handle Mr. Roses' son Noel?

HOW, WITHOUT LOSING CLIENTS, DOES AN ADVISOR MANAGE PEOPLE WHO AGGRESSIVELY ASSERT THEIR POWERS OF ATTORNEY?

There is no guarantee that an advisor will not lose the client. But compromising one's ethical and legal obligations, tarnishing one's reputation, and risking one's license cannot possibly be worth it for any client, no matter how big the account or how good and longstanding a relationship the client and advisor have had. Even in a positive and productive relationship, there is no guarantee that a client will not eventually sue the advisor.

Once the advisor overcomes her fear of losing the client, she will be better equipped to deal with Noel Roses. The advisor should explain to Noel that she, the advisor, has an equal obligation to each of her clients. An advisor would not compromise one client to benefit another. Having to choose between clients would place the advisor in a conflict of interest. The advisor might want to ask Noel how he would feel if the situation was reversed—he was in the hospital and someone else was managing his account and wanted to make changes that the advisor felt were inconsistent with Noel's objectives. What if his sister, the person holding his power of attorney, instructed the advisor to shift the investments so that they were less risky? What if Noel recuperated to find his investments were in Guaranteed Investment Certificates, when he could have been making much better returns? In their conversation, the advisor could tell Noel that it would be her obligation, as Noel's advisor, to protect him from any such changes. The advisor should try to appeal to his sensibilities.

A husband and wife situation can be more difficult to handle because the husband may assert that it is really his money—he may be depositing his earned dollars into his wife's account. It is best for an advisor to set the record straight when Mr. Stevens first instructs him to open an account for his wife. At that point, the advisor will need to explain to Mr. Stevens that as soon as the money is deposited into an account bearing another person's name, Mr. Stevens loses control, even if he is named the power of attorney. That's because the advisor will need to meet the client, Mrs. Stevens, to open the account and set the risk tolerance in accordance with Mrs. Stevens. Her husband, the power of attorney, can adjust his expectations if he understands the rules before opening the account. He will then realize how the account must be managed. Remember, the more an advisor can help clients to manage or adjust their expectations, the less surprised clients will be, and the less likely they will issue a complaint.

Further, allowing the husband to make all of the wife's decisions may ultimately be a mistake, as women are now becoming significant, and sometimes sole, contributors to the family income. To grow a successful business, it is in the advisor's interest to meet and provide quality service to female customers.

At the end of the day, if the person with power of attorney is not persuaded that it is the advisor's legal obligation to service the actual account holder, advisors can blame it on me! They can tell people with powers of attorney that they read this book and learned that they, as advisors, have an obligation to always act in the best interest of clients, even if instructions come from a person with power of attorney. While Noel and Mr. Stevens may be annoyed and even move the accounts, advisors who fulfill their obligations, protect their licenses, reputations, and livelihoods.

SUMMARY

Advisors should reduce their risks by not permitting invisible clients to be ignored. Whether or not people with powers of attorney are well-intentioned, advisors must appreciate that their job is to meet their actual client—the account holder—and to complete the forms that will reflect this person's objectives and risk tolerance, and to ensure investments are suitable.

ADVISORS TAKE ACTION

✓ Distinguish your client from the person who is holding his or her power of attorney.

✓ Do not overlook or underestimate the risk of invisible clients. Ensure that the information on their KYC forms is consistent and that investments are suitable, regardless of who instructs you.

✓ Sensitize yourself to danger signs signaling that the person with power of attorney is acting in his or her own self-interest as opposed to the best interests of the account holder.

✓ Insist that the account be managed in accordance with the named client's goals and objectives rather than the goals and objectives of the person with power of attorney. Even if this insistence means you lose the account, it is a small price to pay for shielding yourself from risk and for protecting your reputation and livelihood.

✓ With regard to husbands and wives, many women are meaningful contributors to the family income and are a good source of business. Minimize your business risks and grow your business by ensuring that you provide proper service to these clients.

CHAPTER 9
Clients and Privacy

I. PRIVACY AND THE OFFICE

Advisors should not expect to have any right to privacy as it relates to information they obtain to operate their businesses. Dealers have a legal and regulatory obligation to supervise all advisors, whether they work independently or are employees. This includes the right to monitor all information contained in an advisor's desk, computer, voice mail, and even briefcase. Of course, dealers should have a written policy to this effect, so that advisors know that in regard to the operation of their businesses, privacy is not an option. The lack of privacy is a necessary consequence of the need for internal controls and supervisory requirements imposed by securities' regulators.

One example of this industry's internal controls and the way in which they cannot allow for advisor privacy at work applies to opening mail. Each office should have internal written policies stating who opens the daily mail. Without such policies and methods to follow, supervisors miss opportunities to identify infractions. These violations increase the risk to the dealer, the advisor, and the entire team.[1]

Many types of letters may arrive at the office every day. There could be a letter from a client with a check payable directly to the advisor, as opposed to the insurance company or dealer. This might be a simple error. I can't tell you how many of my clients have offered to provide me with a check payable to me personally, as opposed to my law firm. Clients don't necessarily understand the connection between lawyers and law firms or advisors and dealers. While the issue of a check

---

1. In some jurisdictions, there are laws that prohibit the opening of mail addressed to others. Therefore, you should consult with a lawyer to determine the appropriate internal policy and how to enforce such policy.

payable to the advisor can be resolved easily, other issues may be more difficult to resolve, for instance; a letter delivered to the office from a client listing a series of concerns or complaints about the product or the advisor. The branch manager or supervisor is obliged to know of all such written complaints or concerns and should not leave it to the advisor to report it up the chain.

Some dealers have policies in place that appoint a single person to open all incoming mail, no matter whose name is on the envelope. This person, usually a supervisor's assistant, date stamps the mail and checks it for possible or actual warning signs. Mail that is identified as potentially problematic is delivered to the supervisor for review and consideration.

The team's reputation is only as good as the individual advisors' reputations, and if one person engages in inappropriate business practices, it can threaten the reputation of the entire team and the dealer. Accordingly, advisors should not expect any privacy at work and should assume that their supervisor, head office, and the regulator are entitled to review all mail, e-mails, letters, and voice mail messages. Of course, if the advisor operates a one-person office, her supervisor should occasionally examine the incoming mail during visits and audits.

Another example of how advisors cannot expect to have privacy relating to work is in regard to their outside business activities and the need to disclose these to dealers. As part of the privilege of having a license to sell in this industry, advisors must be completely transparent to their dealers and regulators and cannot expect any privacy about such matters.

While the advisor has virtually no right to privacy at the office, clients are another story altogether.

II. OBLIGATIONS TO CLIENTS

All professionals must maintain the privacy of information imparted to them by their clients. While the issue of privacy is more prevalent than it's ever been in the working world, maintaining client confidentiality is not new to advisors in the financial and insurance industries. Clients have always been very private about their financial information, and advisors have had to respect their concerns.

Advisors should be aware of specific issues that are now required by law, instead of simply being good business practices. In this chapter, we will briefly review advisors' obligations. The laws vary between jurisdictions, so I will give you general tips and tools that I hope will apply to most jurisdictions. To fine-tune this information, advisors will need to check with their company's privacy officer or with a lawyer in their jurisdiction with expertise in this area.

To succeed as an advisor, it is essential to protect one's clients' personal information. The following is a true story. I went to see an allergist. After poking what seemed to be hundreds of little holes in my arms and inserting small samples of every substance known to mankind, he asked me to meet him in his office. The office had a small desk, two chairs, and a bookshelf. Sounds pretty standard. But every surface of his office had stacks of paper and files. Patients' names were on each file. He invited me to sit down, and I stepped over piles of paper to reach the only clear surface, the chair. He looked up at me and excused himself from the office for a few minutes to talk to his receptionist. While he was away, I had full access to his files, which clearly displayed the names of his clients on each file label. Having no interest whatsoever, I didn't read them.

He returned to his office and asked me if I could wait a moment as he had to dictate an urgent note. He proceeded to dictate a letter, citing the name and address of his patient and her particular medical condition into his handheld tape recorder. I interrupted his dictation and advised him that it was a breach of the patient's privacy rights to have him dictate this information while I was in his office. He responded—and I swear this is what he said—"You don't know her, do you?" Whether or not I knew his patient was completely irrelevant. The patient, just like any professional advisor's client, has a right to the privacy of her personal and medical information.

CLEAN UP THE OFFICE

If advisors meet with clients in the same location where they carry out their duties, their desks must be clear. Clients should not be able to see any files or documentation containing the names and/ or information of other clients, particularly if the advisor leaves the client alone in the office, even if just for a minute.

YOUR COMPUTER, BLACKBERRY®, AND OTHER TECHNO TOYS

I am far from being a computer whiz, but I am aware of some basic privacy concerns:

- Does the advisor's computer have an automatic screen saver? If clients come into an advisor's office, advisors must ensure that the computer screen does not display information concerning other clients. If an advisor leaves the room, even momentarily, she needs to ensure that her computer cannot be accessed by the client in her office. Password protection is highly recommended.
- Does the advisor's hand-held device (BlackBerry®, etc.) have an automatic locking device? Where is the hand-held device stored? Does the hand-held device have password protection? If it does not, and if it is lost or stolen, a breach of privacy will occur.
- Does anyone, other than those in the advisor's office, use her computer or BlackBerry®? I suggest that advisors refrain from allowing relatives or friends to use their computers or any devices that store client information.
- Has the electronic device been encrypted? Encryption is a form of information scrambling, which should preclude a third person from being able to read the contents of intercepted electronic messages. If we send any messages that are not encrypted, we should seek instructions from the client permitting us to send such non-encrypted, unsecured messages.

E-MAILS/MARKETING MATERIALS

Isn't it great that we can e-mail many clients simultaneously? When we do so, however, we need to make sure that the e-mail does not show the names of the other recipients.

SAMPLE STATEMENTS

If an advisor reviews Client A's sample statement while she meets with Client B, she needs to make sure the name and identification, address, and all other identifying information is completely blacked out. Sometimes a document is blacked out, but the information can be seen through the reverse side of the document. Look at both sides of the document to ensure that the client's privacy is maintained.

PAPER PRIVACY

Do advisors have a system to ensure drafts are shredded nightly and faxes don't sit on a public fax tray?

NAME DROPPING

While advisors may be proud of their success, they cannot mention their clients' names or identify any of their clients to others. Many of us try to get clients from our community, club, or neighborhood. We are not permitted to tell a prospect the identity of other clients unless we have express, written permission from the client.

During a client meeting, an advisor's assistant may be tempted to interrupt to address an urgent matter. If the urgency relates to another client, there should be no discussion concerning the matter within earshot of the first client. Instead, the advisor must have this discussion in another room, ensuring no private information can be seen or heard by the client left waiting in the office.

REFERRALS

Advisors may want to share clients with professionals in related businesses, thereby entering into an arrangement in which clients are shared and all professionals profit. Without clients' specific written consent, clients' identities and information cannot be shared. To avoid such breaches of privacy, advisors can display the other professional's business card or provide information about services available to clients.[2]

HOME OFFICES/TAKING WORK HOME FROM THE OFFICE

Daniel Diligent is a very conscientious rookie. He was recently married, and he and his wife purchased their first home, which is

---

2. Ensure the professional is properly licensed and reputable before referring him to your clients, and check with your compliance department to ensure that any terms of referral adhere to the regulations and laws in your jurisdiction and to the company's internal policies.

being built and will be completed in six months. In the meantime, the newlyweds have moved in with the bride's parents.

Most of Daniel's clients are family friends and relatives. Daniel Diligent and his wife share the guest room, which is just big enough for a bed and a closet. At the end of each working day, Daniel leaves the office with a briefcase filled with the following materials:

- notes from meetings, for dictation,
- KYC forms to complete,
- draft agendas to review for meetings scheduled for the following day,
- client monthly statements to review, and
- investment plans he is in the process of completing.

Daniel's in-laws let him work at their living room desk. Daniel is a very hard worker. He arrives at his in-laws' home at 6:00 p.m. most evenings and sets up the desk in the living room so that he can begin his evening work immediately after dinner. He takes a shower, has a delicious dinner, and gets down to work.

Violations?

Do Daniel's clients expect him to leave personal financial information where his wife and her parents can see it? What if neighbors, friends, or family visit? If advisors take work home, they cannot leave it in open view of anyone who is at home or may come in—family members, neighbors, friends, children, domestic and other workers, and so on. To leave personal financial information in the open violates privacy laws and the privacy policies of most companies.

How would a relative who was also a client feel if she came for a visit and saw her personal information in full view? Many people have home offices or take work home at night or on weekends. If private information is removed from the office, advisors must ensure that it remains securely away from family, friends, and the public at all times.

Tips For Advisors:

- Do not leave your briefcase at a public coat check when stopping on the way home for a drink or dinner.
- Do not leave your briefcase in the car—car thieves thrive in many towns and cities.
- Anytime you are in public, including while commuting to and from work and appointments, refrain from using your cellular telephone or BlackBerry® or from reviewing confidential client documents: others may overhear your conversations or see private client information.
- Do not work on a table in your kitchen or dining room, where people, including family or others with whom you live, can see your files. It breaches your clients' rights to privacy if people who do not work in your office have access to private client information. If you plan to work at home and do not keep all materials in a locked briefcase when not using them, ensure the room in which you leave the materials can be locked from the outside. That way no one else can view the private information. Visualize a neighbor or relative dropping in to visit and observing details of your client's personal holdings. Even setting aside the issue of your legal obligations to keep client information private, imagine the effect on the visitor of this breach of privacy. Such an occurrence would not instill certainty that you maintain the confidentiality of client information—quite the opposite, in fact.
- If you have a self-contained home office, a room where you keep client files, you will need locked filing cabinets.
- Keep a shredder in your home office so that you can shred any discarded confidential information. Otherwise, in your briefcase, keep a file for materials to be discarded at the office, and shred them when you return to the office.

I do very little client work at home. Instead, home is where I do a lot of my writing and catch up on my reading. I bring stacks of materials home and throw them out after I read them because they are regulatory bulletins or magazines and articles that are available to the public. This means I don't have to worry about shredding, even though we have a shredder at home.

GOSSIP

Over the years, I have noticed that keeping secrets means something different to different people. I am the youngest of four children. When I was a child, my siblings would threaten my life if I dared to breathe a word of their mischief to our parents. I am deeply grateful for their teachings. I never tell. As my friends say, "Once you tell Ellen something, it is locked in the vault." Clients have a right to 100 percent privacy. I never tell anyone any business about my clients, and advisors should never reveal anything about their clients.

EXCEPTIONS

In some of the following circumstances, a client's privacy is not maintained; although such exceptions may vary between jurisdictions:

- Client sues—When the client sues an advisor, dealer, or insurance company, the advisor can use any of the client's private information to defend herself or her dealer. Then, the advisor should give all client information and documentation to her lawyer or her dealer's lawyer.
- Dealers and insurance companies—Dealers and insurance companies have regulatory obligations to supervise advisors and may be legally responsible for the services provided by their advisors.[3]
- Regulator calls—Regulators are entitled to private information. In fact, in most jurisdictions, the advisor is compelled to co-operate with the regulator and must provide all documentation requested, even if it is confidential. Advisors should, however, check with their compliance departments before handing over such information.
- Subpoena or court order—If the advisor receives a court-issued subpoena, the advisor will likely be legally obligated to adhere to its terms. The advisor will need to retain a

---

3. The legal concept is referred to as "vicarious liability," but this topic is beyond the scope of this book.

lawyer to determine that the subpoena is legitimate and to receive legal advice on his or her rights and obligations. If the advisor's dealer has an in-house lawyer, the advisor will need to send the subpoena to him or her to review before providing any documentation. That's because any breach of privacy by the advisor may also jeopardize the dealer.

In many cases, the subpoena gives the advisor a specific date and time at which to appear in a certain courtroom with the documents. The advisor will want to know in advance whether the party sending him the subpoena wants him to testify or if they just want the documents. If they only want documentation, then the advisor will need to seek counsel to determine whether he can just send the documentation or whether he must appear. If, however, one of the parties to the legal proceedings wants the advisor to testify, then the advisor will need to appear with counsel to protect his and his dealer's interests.

A common example is when a client is engaged in divorce proceedings and the husband or wife involves the advisor or his dealer. Another typical example is if there are collection proceedings against one's client and the collector subpoenas the advisor for evidence concerning the assets in the accounts and whether such assets have recently been transferred to another location.

There are taxes, trusts, wills, and estate proceedings that may also involve the advisor's testimony. Advisors should remember that if they receive a subpoena or court order, they should notify their dealer and get legal support and advice before appearing in court or delivering documentation.

- Consent or direction by the client—Typically, consent may be provided orally or in writing; consent may be given directly or it may be implied. But, in this industry, I strongly recommend that the information not be disclosed to any third party without a clear, written direction signed by the client. A common example is when a client directs an advisor to supply information to his accountant or his lawyer. In such circumstances, written consent and direction is necessary. Anything short of written consent leaves the advisor vulnerable to allegations of breach of a client's privacy. If the advisor must send documentation or impart information to a third party, advisors should obtain specific, written consent rather than relying on a standard form previously signed by the client, with a privacy consent embedded in minuscule writing.

If advisors receive a signed consent or written permission to provide a particular individual with private information, and such information is being picked up from the advisor's office, they should ask for identification from the person who comes to retrieve the information. This is to confirm that they are providing the information to the right person. Then, advisors should photocopy the identification and put it in the file along with the consent.

Sometimes when clients sign forms for dealers and insurance companies, the forms include a direction for the dealer and/or insurance company to provide private information in response to a potential future request from the client. To be sure that the client has read and understood the privacy provision, it is wise to point out the clause and have the client initial the particular clause confirming that she read and understood that she waives certain rights to privacy. If circumstances arise and the advisor is uncertain whether the client anticipated that a waiver or previously signed consent would be used in these circumstances, then it is recommended that the client sign a new form or agreement to confirm approval. Advisors should always explain the reason for the request for the consent and what is intended, if private information is being delivered to someone other than the client.

Situations arise which can create big problems. Advisors complain that sons and daughters want access to an elderly parent's money. They want information, allegedly for the accountant or for payment to their parents' caregivers. In those situations, the advisor, who wants to do what is best for the client, is tempted to share information with the son or daughter.

The situation can become even more complicated when the client has been to the advisor's office on many occasions with this adult child, and the advisor's impression was that the mother trusted her child. The advisor may also truly believe that the son or daughter intends well, but one never knows. If the advisor is not absolutely certain that he has the necessary written consent from the account holder, the client, he should consult with the in-house legal or compliance departments. Although perhaps unlikely, what if the son or daughter uses the money for his or her own benefit? All attention will turn to the advisor and dealer in an effort to reimburse the client or the client's other beneficiaries.

SUMMARY

Company policies regarding privacy are extremely important for an advisor to understand and comply with. Having policies in place for tasks like opening mail, and ensuring that only appropriate tasks are delegated, makes an advisor's practice more professional. Maintaining a client's privacy and anonymity is especially important to the advisor's practice and success if a complaint is ever made against him.

ADVISORS TAKE ACTION

✓ Read and understand the internal privacy policies mandated by your dealer and regulator.

✓ Do not expect to have any privacy in regard to your own correspondence delivered from or to your office.

✓ To reduce advisor and dealer risk, it is necessary to have policies that permit opening all incoming mail.

✓ Ensure that your personal practices when removing client information from the office or when working from a home office adhere to dealers' privacy policies and the laws of the jurisdiction.

✓ There are exceptions to privacy that may be unique in each jurisdiction.

✓ Protect clients' personal information unless an exception applies or a client has consented in writing.

✓ If you believe that an exception applies, get necessary legal advice to ensure that you comply appropriately.

CHAPTER 10
Compliance — Friend or Foe?

Advisors are waking up to the obligations inherent in this highly regulated environment, an environment where a breach of privacy, ethics, rules, and regulations can end a career faster than you can say "K-Y-C." Until recently, most advisors didn't appreciate the importance of the compliance officer's role. Rather than relying on these people for support, they treated them as the enemy.

Dealers are required by law to hire compliance officers, who are responsible for supervising trades and regularly sending memos and/or e-mails alerting advisors to potential violations. Advisors and dealers who want to build a business and manage compliance risks have realized that compliance departments are a necessary resource.

When advisors and branch managers identify a danger signal or a potential compliance problem, they can turn to compliance officers for an answer. Having such a resource enables advisors, supervisors, and dealers to successfully withstand challenges and stay in business over the long run.

Advisors and branch managers should not, however, be lulled into a false sense of security—relying exclusively on compliance officers to alert them to danger. Compliance officers do not meet clients, and they are not in the branch every day observing the advisors and branch managers. As a result, it is not always possible for the compliance department to catch problems before they arise. In this chapter, I will explain how the advisor and branch manager should respond to inquiries from compliance and how they can be proactive about maintaining, rather than breaching, compliance procedures. This way, advisors and branch managers don't need to rely too heavily on head office to identify compliance problems.

I. WHEN COMPLIANCE RAISES THE RED FLAG

How do compliance officers become aware of potential infractions? It may be from electronic trade reviews or from branch audits, in which branch files are reviewed and errors are discovered before the client or regulator recognizes a potential problem.

What should advisors do when the compliance department raises the red flag? How should advisors react to such memos? First, do not take it personally. Regardless of how a problem is identified, a message from the compliance department may alert an advisor to an infraction early enough that the advisor may be able to fix the problem before it grows and/or comes to the client's or regulator's attention. For example, in the story of Mr. Roses in Chapter 8, a compliance officer may have e-mailed the advisor after receiving the updated KYC form increasing the risk tolerance of the elderly client. The form may have been processed, but with a query from the compliance department. If the advisor ignores the e-mail and trades in more speculative investments that lose money, the advisor could be at greater risk of getting a complaint from a client or of facing litigation. Advisors and branch managers who ignore compliance officers' concerns and recommendations should expect trouble when the regulator audits or the client complains. If there is evidence that the advisor and branch manager ignored problems identified by the compliance department, these individuals can expect much greater penalties, including suspension, loss of license, or more.

Remember, regulators can choose to audit any dealer's branch whenever they like. Regulators are entitled to review and obtain copies, or originals if they wish, of any documents. If a client complains, the regulators request copies of all internal correspondence, including e-mail exchanges between compliance officers and the advisor or branch manager. As part of its investigation, the regulator will also get copies of all correspondence between the advisor and compliance officers. No response or a rude response from an advisor will provide evidence for the regulator and client that their allegations of the advisor's disregard for the compliance department were correct. In short, the possible consequences for an advisor who ignores the recommendations of compliance officers may be many: increased penalties; revocation or suspension of an advisor's license; litigation, and a damaged reputation.

What happens after the compliance department raises a red flag, and it appears that an advisor committed an infraction, advertently or inadvertently? At that point, a compliance officer may tell the advisor that the compliance department will need to impose an internal form of discipline on him. While this may upset the advisor, such steps may actually protect him. How? When the regulator performs its audit, it will observe that the dealer already dealt with an infraction. Sometimes, when the infraction has been sufficiently dealt with internally, the regulator does not impose an additional penalty, as the matter has been satisfactorily concluded.

Accordingly, when the compliance officer inquires about a trade, the branch manager and advisor should respond by first thanking the compliance officer. A disproportionate number of complaints and claims are based on allegations of unsuitability. Many trade inquiries are prompted because the trade is inconsistent with the information contained in the KYC form. If such inconsistency can be proven, the client may succeed in a complaint. But if the compliance officer issues an inquiry before the client complains, advisors should consider themselves fortunate. This gives advisors an opportunity to resolve the issue either by adjusting the investments or by changing the stated objectives, but only if appropriate—advisors should not forget the Triangle of Suitability that was discussed in Chapter 4.

II. BE PROACTIVE

As suggested above, compliance officers cannot look over every advisor and branch manager's shoulder every minute of every day. Therefore, advisors must not rely on compliance officers to uncover every potential infraction. Advisors need to sensitize themselves to issues that arise, so that they can identify problems before they occur, even if these problems were not identified by compliance staff. With regulatory scrutiny being what it is today, advisors and dealers should be motivated to guard against violating the rules of compliance. Advisors, branch managers, and dealers are well advised to perform the necessary due diligence to determine whether those with whom they are affiliated value a culture of compliance.

To ensure that they are complying and not risking compliance violations, advisors and dealers need to know what to look for. The following roadmap lists issues to explore and questions to ask.

Is a dealer's policies and procedures manual integral to the dealer's operations?

> Red light answers: "We can't locate it; it's outdated, buried, or not easily accessible."

Firms that value ethics and integrity will withstand the scrutiny of regulators and the complaints of clients' lawyers. These firms will survive and grow in the long term.

The dealer's policies and procedures manual is an important item to protect dealers and advisors. The policies in the manual are specifically designed for the internal operations of the firm. The mere existence of policies is one thing. Adhering to those policies and ensuring that they are followed and become integral to how the company operates is more challenging.

All participants in this industry—from the most senior to the most junior executives—need to ensure that a compliance culture exists that is intrinsic to everyone working with the dealer. That means everyone, including the CEO and president, senior management, and all advisors, adheres to compliance requirements that extend beyond what is written in the policies and procedures' manual.

Judges and regulators will examine the dealer's operations to determine whether the advisors adhere to set policies. These policies are the standards by which judges and regulators measure the firm. Whether or not the firm's policies were adhered to is one element that is examined to determine whether the firm met its legal and regulatory obligations.

> Green Light Answer: "On the desk of each licensed and unlicensed person, or accessible on the dealer's intranet and updated regularly, is a copy of the company policy. Mandatory training is provided to advisors on an ongoing basis by the dealer, which is committed to continually investing in education."

Having this policy in easy reach shows that a firm values the ethics set by senior management, ethics which permeate the firm.

Who supervises and what reviews are done daily and monthly?

Red Light Answers: "The branch manager is out of the office most of the time, so his assistant assumes all his responsibilities."
"I don't know; I think it must be Joe."
"I think it is someone at head office."
"We have it great—it is Frank, but no one respects him, so we just ignore his inquiries."
"It is Joe—I am not sure what he does—you will need to ask him, but good luck getting him off the phone with his own clients."

The branch manager is the first line of defense for the advisor. Without a diligent supervisor, the advisor is vulnerable to his own breaches and the breaches of others in the branch. The branch manager must review accounts before they are opened and must review trades and commissions regularly. If such reviews are not diligently completed, then the branch may be subject to audits, reviews, and ultimately to bad publicity if there are enforcement proceedings. Cautious advisors will ask their branch managers specific questions concerning their daily and monthly routines to ensure that internal policy obligations are met and surpassed.

Advisors should pay attention to their own impressions of the branch manager. What are the branch manager's values? Does the manager have his own book of business? How much time does he spend on managing? How much time is spent on growing and managing his own book? Does he operate the largest book in the branch? If so, he may have been promoted because of his successful sales and not because of his management ability. Does the branch manager have regular meetings with advisors? Are the following such topics on the agenda: managing the firm, compliance, and training? Do specialized speakers or coaches come in to help the group with obstacles?

Compliance is the second-tier defense. It is often described as "second-tier supervision." Advisors should ask about the compliance officer responsible for that branch and how much contact and correspondence there is between the compliance officer and the advisors. Do branch managers and advisors try to work with the compliance department to resolve looming issues before they result in compliance problems or lawsuits?

> Green Light Answer: "It is Joe and you had better respond to him when he makes inquiries because he doesn't mess around with compliance. He reviews our trades every day and he asks questions—it's a pain but, in the long run, it's good because we have a clean branch. The branch I was at before spent hours following up with audit reviews by the regulator and had several client complaints that brought the entire branch down."

How many client complaints are on file at any given time, and what are the most common complaints?

> Red Light Answer: "The branch manager doesn't have a file. I am not sure how many there are—I have about three, and I think the other advisors have a few, but they are without merit. Oh, I almost forgot, the branch manager has also been hauled in by the regulator for his own trades as well as for failure to supervise."[1]

The number of enforcement proceedings against the advisors in any one branch is a barometer of whether or not the branch is compliant. Are there many complaints? Have any such complaints succeeded against the advisor, branch manager, and/or dealer?

> Green Light Answer: "We are proud that we have had only one complaint in the past two years, and it was dismissed as it had no merit. Otherwise, our branch has a clean bill of health."

---

1. Note that in most jurisdictions, branch managers are required to have a file containing all client complaints. Branch managers who don't have such a file may be in breach of regulatory obligations.

Do advisors know what to do when faced with a client complaint?

Red Light Answer: "Try to settle with the client quickly and privately. Whatever you do, don't tell anyone and hope that the entire problem just goes away."

In most jurisdictions, it is a regulatory infraction to settle the matter directly with the client. Further, a direct settlement with the client will likely not include obtaining a release from the client. Without the release, the advisor and dealer may be exposed to a string of complaints from the same client, who can use the previous settlement to induce the advisor to pay him more money. It is a very slippery slope, and very dangerous for an advisor to settle directly with a client.

Some advisors feel compelled to apologize without benefit of an independent assessment of the client's complaint. This is dangerous because the client will have evidence of the advisor's admission of breach. For advisors who have errors and omissions insurance, any admission of liability may lead the insurance provider to deny coverage of the claim. Advisors should remember that just because they like a client and feel badly about a loss, it doesn't mean that they have breached any obligations.

Green Light Answer: "I know to keep calm and politely ask the client to provide a written complaint. I call my branch manager and compliance officer and tell them what happened. If the complaint letter arrives, I give it to the branch manager and compliance officer immediately. No matter what happens, I don't admit, deny, or blame others."

When the dealer recruits, what questions are asked?

Red Light Answer: "We ask the only question that matters—how big is your book?"

More than size matters when reviewing an advisor's book of business. It would worry me if a firm focuses exclusively on the gross

145

value of an advisor's book, ignoring its quality. After all, a high-risk advisor can sink the reputation of an entire firm.

When interviewing a candidate for the role of advisor, the dealer is well advised to review the risk in the advisor's book. If the dealer does not check the quality of the advisor's book of business before agreeing to hire her, the dealer may be assuming a big risk for the firm.

The Internet is a tool that can be used to determine whether the advisor has been the subject of a regulatory disciplinary hearing or settlement in the past several years. While a couple of small infractions are not necessarily a problem, more than one serious matter may reveal a systemic problem. Some advisors, however, may have been investigated for infractions minor enough that they kept their licenses. This is a topic to explore with the advisor.

> Green Light Answer: "When the branch manager or head office recruits, we ask questions to determine the true value of the book, including how much of the advisor's book comes from clients borrowing to invest, commonly referred to as leverage loans."

Does the office seem compliant?

> Red Light Answer: "Well, it is a mess with no semblance of order at all. There are no filing cabinets, so files are stacked all over the place: on the floor, on the desks, in the hallways. I don't know how they find anything, but I am sure they are compliant, because they say they are."

What general impression do people receive upon entering the office? How are clients greeted as they arrive? Are the offices tidy and are most files stored in locked cabinets? Or, are there stacks of paper and files on the floor and on desks, which could be read by any visitor, in violation of privacy laws?

> Green Light Answer: "My overall impression is that the office operates in a professional manner. It is tidy and the way in which information is stored prohibits one from seeing clients' names or identification."

What is the dealer's policy on alternative products?

Red Light Answer: "I have no idea; I just sell them."

What are the internal procedures for approving such products? Are many of the branch's clients heavily invested in alternative products? While these products may be good quality, there may be stringent regulatory requirements concerning the approval of these products. The regulatory requirements may also extend to qualifying the people to whom such products can be sold. Advisors will want to satisfy themselves that regulations are being followed and that the dealer provides appropriate support in the form of product training, guidance on risk disclosure, and suitability.

Green Light Answer: "There are strict policies. Head office reviews the product and performs its due diligence. Then, only if the product is placed on the dealer's list of acceptable products to sell, may we sell to clients who qualify and for whom the product is suitable—and this is only after we get the necessary training."

What is the dealer's view of documenting files?

Red Light Answer: "We never worry too much as long as there is some form of KYC in the file."

Examine the forms used by the dealer and ascertain when they were last updated and whether they comply with various obligations, including anti-money laundering. Do the advisors in the branch keep their KYC forms updated, and what is the dealer's policy? Are the advisors in the habit of keeping notes of meetings and telephone conversations, and what methodology is used? Is there software available that is used throughout the branch or dealer's office?

Green Light Answer: "This is a high priority. I document every telephone call and meeting. I use a form that the author of this great book put in Chapter 6, which sets out the time and date of the call or meeting, who I am speaking to, and what was discussed. If the meeting is in my office, I sometimes type the information directly into a terrific software program that I have, so that if I am not in the office when the client calls, others on my team can follow what was previously discussed."

How is compliance viewed in this branch and in the firm?

Red Light Answers: "We hate compliance and we ignore any inquiries and hope they disappear."
"Compliance is a real pain—they keep hounding us, but our branch manager deals with it for us, and they seem to disappear, as he is the firm's biggest producer, and they won't mess with him."
"Compliance is evil and I hate them; they never leave us alone. It's as if they have it out for our branch. Every day it is something else—a new memo or bulletin. Who has the time to read it all?" (At least this answer indicates that head office is aware of compliance issues in the branch and will not let them continue to operate unless they resolve the issues.)

Are compliance officers perceived as police who only come in with guns loaded when something goes wrong, or are they regarded as an integral support to the operation of the business? If the compliance department is not viewed as a partner in the organization, the firm might face serious problems in the near future. Is the compliance team solid, and is it respected by all of the firm's managers?

Green Light Answer: "Our advisors, branch manager, and head office take compliance seriously and that ensures that the branch manager has the time and energy to mentor us and help us grow our books of business."

These are only some of the issues that advisors will want to examine in order to ascertain the dealer's professionalism and to protect their own business risk. Advisors should do their own mini-audit by asking themselves these questions and examining these issues. These days no one can afford to ignore the compliance department. This means advisors will want to gauge whether the organization values its regulatory obligations.

What if compliance is ignored? With non-compliant dealers and branches, the risk increases substantially as one of, several, or all of the branch clients may sue, either separately, as a group, or by class action. By the time the first complaint or action commences, the red flag is waving so brightly, it is too late to resolve problems without significant cost.

III. COMPLIANCE BEFORE HIRING

Dealers and branch managers who value compliance will want to protect their businesses by ensuring that they only recruit and hire advisors who are not at risk. Advisors should be prepared to be scrutinized when applying to join a new dealer. Here are the issues that will be examined:

VALUE OF ADVISOR'S BOOK

Is the value of the advisor's book of business based on borrowed money through margin accounts or through a leverage loan program? If so, what is the ratio of borrowed money to real money? Did the clients sign documentation for leverage loan disclosure or margin account agreements? Does the advisor have a record of explaining to clients the risks of borrowing to invest?

SOUND BUSINESS PRACTICES

What does the advisor do to understand her clients' objectives and risk tolerance? What processes are in place to ascertain what is suitable for each client? Does the advisor follow a method or process? Does the advisor maintain a paper trail? Do dealers know about an advisor's paper trails only by asking about them, or do dealers ask to see any templates or tools used by the advisor?

PRODUCTS

What products does an advisor follow and what due diligence does she engage in to ensure she understands the products and their risks? Does the advisor follow the investments, and how frequently does she call clients to update them?

DEBT ISSUES

Through a questionnaire or dialogue, the recruiting company may ask the advisor about past judgments, garnishments, and bankruptcies. The recruiting company may obtain some information from bankruptcy, newspaper, and Internet searches, all of which are public. To do a credit search, the company may need to obtain the advisor's written permission, depending upon the laws of the jurisdiction. This issue is important. Many people believe that if an advisor does not have her own financial affairs in order, she should not be managing other people's money.

REGULATORY OR LITIGATION PROBLEMS OR COMPLAINTS

An advisor should be questioned and her responses noted on past regulatory problems. Has she encountered problems through regulators or through internal discipline? Has she had to defend herself against litigation? I encourage advisors to disclose this information up front because, no matter what, the dealer will uncover these facts through searching. Dishonesty significantly reduces an advisor's chance to obtain an offer of employment.

OUTSIDE BUSINESS ACTIVITIES

Does the advisor have any outside business activities to report? If the advisor accepts a position with the dealer, she will need to inform the company and seek permission to continue any outside business activities. In any event, it is better if the dealer knows about the advisor's intentions up front. That way, before being hired, the advisor will know whether she can continue her other work if she gets the position.

REASONS FOR LEAVING THE OTHER DEALER

Why is the advisor leaving her dealer? If the answer to this question doesn't emerge in discussions with the new dealer and prospective employee, the question will be asked. Other necessary questions to ask an advisor looking for a new position include the following: Is the advisor still registered with a dealer? If she is not still registered with a dealer, what were the circumstances of termination? Obtaining a copy of the Uniform Termination Notice

(UTN) will reveal whether the advisor was terminated for cause or whether other issues were registered with the regulator through the filing of the UTN.

HOW DOES THE ADVISOR INTEND TO BRING CLIENTS OVER?

What is the advisor's obligation to her current dealer? Does she have a written contract? If so, the new dealer will want to see a copy. How does the advisor intend to leave her current dealer? Will it be professionally and by the book, or—bad news!—has she removed documentation from her current dealer that she was legally forbidden to remove?

Here is an example of what the advisor should *not* do when she plans to leave her current dealer:

Daniel Diligent wants to change dealers. He decides that before he begins his new job search, he will copy all his client information (KYC forms and client contact information) and take it to his in-laws' home, where he will store it in the basement.

He will also e-mail private client information to a Hotmail® account he set up on his father-in-law's computer.

After all this is done, he begins his job search. Using the BlackBerry® supplied by his dealer, he sends and receives e-mails to and from his recruiter. Oops! These are now on the company's system.

Without providing any advance notice, he tells his employer he is leaving to work for another dealer.

Let's examine the advisor's violations:

Clients do not anticipate that Daniel will store their personal information in his in-laws' basement. This is a clear breach of privacy, which may end up in a complaint.

E-mails can be detected, even if delivered several months before, because they may remain on the company's computer system after they have been deleted.

Hotmail® accounts do not have the same security as the dealer's network. Regardless of how the tug of war between the dealer and the departing advisor turns out, clients are entitled to an advisor who has done everything possible to secure their personal information.

Documentation belongs to the company unless an exception has been specified in a written agreement. What if the dealer being left by the advisor sues the advisor? In that case, the trial judge will examine the relationship between advisor and dealer, paying close attention to all written contracts to determine whether the departing advisor has breached any legal obligations to the company he is leaving. The judge will scrutinize the behaviour of all parties throughout their relationship, to ascertain any unwritten legal obligations. Before resigning, advisors should obtain legal advice to determine if they have any obligations to the dealer they will be leaving.

While this is not a comprehensive list of issues a dealer would review through the hiring process, the advisor can appreciate that a compliant recruiting company will be interested in information that goes far beyond basic questions about the size of her business. Before shopping for a new dealer, the advisor is well advised to ensure her book is compliant.

IV.   ADVISOR OR COMPLIANCE DRIVEN?

Advisor Driven: When the compliance department refuses to process a trade, the advisor may have the clout to convince senior management to override the compliance officer's decision. If dealers fear losing an advisor—particularly a big producer—to their competitors, they may succumb to the advisor's wishes. In the process, they risk their advisor's reputation and their own. With regulators not hesitating to issue significant penalties and lengthy suspensions, this is a dangerous way for dealers to work. For a single complaint, the advisor pays a huge personal price and substantial legal fees. I suggest that an advisor-driven firm will enjoy the growth of its business in the short term but, in the long run, the firm could pay a huge price. Revenues may increase at first, but eventually expenses will increase for the following reasons: legal fees, payment to clients to reimburse them for losses if investments were unsuitable, regulatory penalties, and the opportunity costs described in Chapter 1. As the advisor's stress level goes up, his revenue and reputation go down. Instead, I suggest that firms, dealers, and advisors consider becoming compliance driven.

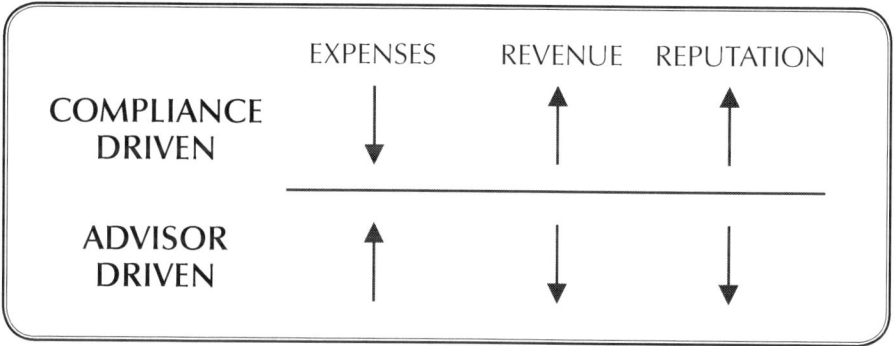

Compliance Driven: Firms that are compliance driven will adhere to the compliance officer's suggestions. This way, neither the reputation of the firm and its staff nor regulatory and legal obligations are compromised. Compliance-driven firms will certainly not compromise for the sake of keeping, rather than losing, producers who are among their "biggest" but not their "best" advisors. I say "biggest" and "not best" because the best producers will only want to join dealers with great reputations. It's possible that a dealer's revenue may suffer in the short run if certain big producers leave for less compliant competitors. In the long run, however, the firm will rise to the top, attracting strong and compliant advisors who value reputation and a strong compliance department.

Most advisors do not appreciate the different functions of compliance departments. So what do compliance departments do? Their many duties include registrations; reviews of marketing material to ensure that advisors don't run afoul of the misleading prohibitions; trade and suitability reviews; conflict-of-interest management; and so on. All these compliance responsibilities are key to advisors maintaining a clean and profitable business. Compliance is not an advisor's enemy. Instead, the compliance department is the most valuable resource given to advisors by the dealer. It's there to help advisors protect their business. If you are an advisor, use it.

SUMMARY

No doubt about it, advisors want to avoid client complaints and investigations. Even one complaint can tarnish an advisor's reputation, threaten his right to a license, and hurt his bottom line. In some ways then, an advisor's best line of defense is the compliance department. This helpful resource can steer advisors away from potential danger. Advisors benefit both financially and professionally when they understand how they can protect themselves when compliance identifies a problem. Using compliance as a resource also decreases client complaints.

ADVISORS TAKE ACTION

✓ Use compliance as a resource.

✓ Make changes that will pass the scrutiny of a regulatory review and that will be less likely to provoke complaints from clients.

✓ Don't fear losing a client.

✓ Act on the compliance officer's memos.

✓ Remain compliance driven.

✓ Perform the necessary due diligence including taking notes on the book of business maintained, alternative products offered, dealer policies, and the competency and professionalism of the office.

✓ Look for red flags and decide accordingly; carefully assess the branch manager, the compliance department, and the dealer's values.

✓ If a recruiting company interviews you for a new position, be prepared to honestly answer questions about your habits, processes, and procedures. Remember that companies want advisors who will increase their profitability and not their compliance risk.

✓ Protect your license, your livelihood, and your reputation as a professional. One way to do this is to choose a firm that values compliance.

CHAPTER 11
The Litigation Process—Summary

This book does not purport to be an authority on the process of litigation. Entire books are written on the subject, and advisors and dealers are well advised to seek advice from lawyers practicing in their particular jurisdiction.

Most jurisdictions have the following stages to each proceeding, but the rules in each jurisdiction vary. We will first review what clients want, who they sue, and other decisions made before they begin litigation.

BEFORE LITIGATION:

WHAT DO CLIENTS WANT?

Clients want money. The difficulty is that clients are often unrealistic about the sum lost because of the alleged breach, and they don't realize, until well into the litigation, that the cost of litigation, along with the aggravation, may outweigh the sum they ultimately collect. Clients must pass through several expensive procedural and legal challenges, after which there is no guarantee that they will get their money back.

WHERE DO CLIENTS COMMENCE PROCEEDINGS?
In Court

Certain services in North American banking and investment industries offer dispute resolution before a claim is made in court. Failing such resolutions, however, clients sue their advisors and dealers if the goal is to get their money back. Legal proceedings commence by issuing and filing documents in court that set out the allegations and the sum sought to be collected from each party. In some jurisdictions, regulators lack the authority to order reimbursement for losses to the client, so if that is the client's goal,

155

a complaint to the regulator will likely not serve this purpose. Regulators may penalize the advisor if there is a regulatory breach and may suspend or revoke the advisor's license. How can a client legally compel an advisor or dealer to reimburse him for his losses? In many jurisdictions, a client can only do this by beginning court proceedings.

JURISDICTION

The party suing is called the plaintiff. Plaintiffs can choose the jurisdiction in which to commence the action. Usually, the jurisdiction chosen is the one where the client lives. It can be difficult for the advisor to successfully challenge the choice of jurisdiction and compel the plaintiff/client to move the claim to a jurisdiction that would be more convenient for the advisor and/or dealer. Of course, occasionally, an advisor may wish he was not being sued in his own jurisdiction. If the advisor lives in the same small town as his client, he may worry about gossip arising from the claim, which will damage his reputation.

SETTLEMENT BEFORE LITIGATION

Sometimes the matter is settled before documents are drafted and filed with the court. Some advisors complain that their dealers are too quick to settle. I suggest, however, that most dealers take a broader approach and are sufficiently experienced to know that if the proceedings are likely to substantially damage reputations, it may be better to settle the matter and have the client sign a release containing a confidentiality clause that compels her to keep all aspects of the settlement completely confidential.

In most jurisdictions, the settlement cannot prohibit the client from complaining to the regulator. In fact, even suggesting the inclusion of a term that prohibits the client from complaining to the regulator can get the advisor in trouble with the regulator. After including such terms in a client release, dealers and advisors have been hauled in by regulators for questioning. No release or settlement term can preclude clients from launching regulatory complaints after they receive settlement funds.

Sometimes, advisors would very much like to settle the case

with the client before informing the dealer, but this is a regulatory breach. Even if it were not, it is dangerous for the advisor to pay the client in hope that the matter will disappear. That's because the client will come to expect the advisor to reimburse her each time she suffers losses. Paying the client in this way is a bad precedent and can be costly to the advisor whose clients know one another. News spreads quickly and other clients will begin to nag until they, too, are reimbursed for losses. One nagging client is bad enough, but an entire client base that operates in this fashion will undoubtedly end the advisor's career.

WHO DO CLIENTS SUE?

Every Party In The Chain

Lawyers advise their clients to identify every party and entity in the chain of companies and individuals linked to the purchase of the product. If the loss is in regard to an insurance product, the client will likely sue the insurance company, with which she has a contract; the agent and the company that pays commissions to the agent; the broker; and any entity that serves as middleman between the insurance company and the agent.[1]

If the claim is for securities' losses, the client will sue the advisor and her dealer. Certain types of advisors can be paid through incorporated companies; those companies would likely also be sued.

Deep Pockets

Lawyers advise their clients to sue every party in the chain, particularly those with "deep pockets." By following this advice, successful plaintiffs can collect from the defendants.

If the parties do not own assets sufficient to satisfy the sum of the judgment, the client will be stuck with a worthless judgment. Knowing that the advisor may not own any assets registered under his own name, rendering him judgment proof, the client usually sues the dealer. Of course, in jurisdictions in which the advisor

---

1.   Insurance broker, Managing General Agent (MGA), Associate General Agent (AGA)

collects commissions directly, clients probably could collect on their judgments by obtaining a portion of the commissions paid to the advisor over time.

WHEN DO CLIENTS SUE?

Limitation Period

Most jurisdictions have legislation that imposes a limit on the time period that can pass after clients have suffered losses. Once this time period, referred to as a "limitation period," is over, clients lose their right to sue. The limitation period varies between jurisdictions and may also depend upon the nature of the claim.

There may also be a limitation period associated with a regulatory complaint. However, this, too, varies depending upon the jurisdiction and the specific regulatory framework.

COMMENCEMENT OF THE PROCEEDINGS:

EXCHANGE OF PLEADINGS

The client can only sue her advisor if she has a legal reason to do so. In other words, a client cannot just sue because she lost money. There must be a fault associated with the loss for which the client can turn to the advisor. Often, clients allege that the advisor breached his duty to them. The most common allegation is that the advisor recommended unsuitable investments. This is usually accompanied by the allegation that the advisor breached his duty by failing to properly know the client. The client may also allege that she didn't provide the advisor with instructions to sell or buy the particular investment. There may also be allegations that the advisor put his own interests ahead of the client's, either by choosing investments with greater commissions for advisors or by trading more frequently than appropriate, thereby generating more commissions, commonly referred to as churning.

The plaintiff's (client's) lawyer prepares a document that sets out the amount of damages sought and specifies the facts needed by the plaintiff to prove her case. This document is the basis of the plaintiff's claim but does not provide full particulars; those are obtained later in the process. The information in the claim must only support the basis in law upon which the plaintiff builds her case. This claim is usually the first document the trial judge reads before the trial begins. The plaintiff's lawyer usually takes this opportunity, therefore, to describe the client in sympathetic terms.

After they have received the claim, the dealer and advisor respond to the claim in writing through a document called a Statement of Defense. If the advisor continues to be registered with the dealer at the time of the claim, the advisor and dealer can usually retain the same lawyer if there are no conflicts between their respective positions. This is much more economical than using different lawyers. On the other hand, if the advisor's and dealer's interests diverge, or if the advisor has left the industry or is registered through another dealer, each party may retain their own lawyer.

The Statement of Defense responds to the allegations in the claim, denying the plaintiff's allegations and describing the advisor's own version of events. For example, the client may allege that she told the advisor she was going to rely on this money for her retirement and, therefore, the highly speculative investments were unsuitable. The advisor may respond by denying that the client intended to rely on this money for retirement and by asserting that the investment was only medium risk and that the plaintiff was a sophisticated investor who told the advisor that 30-to-45 percent medium- to high-risk investments in her account was acceptable. To show that the client had been willing to assume some risk, the advisor and his lawyer would refer to information in the KYC form.

DOCUMENTARY EXCHANGE

In most jurisdictions, after exchanging statements of claim and defense, the parties must exchange documentation relevant to the claim and defense. The parties to the proceeding cannot pick and choose which documents to deliver to their opponent. Documents, whether they are detrimental or helpful to the party's case, must be delivered.

Although this is the first time the opponents—the client and the advisor—obtain documentation from each other, it is not the first time each lawyer sees her own client's documents. In fact, the earlier in the process each party's lawyer sees her own client's documents, the better it is for each client. To draft a proper pleading, whether it is a claim for the plaintiff or a defense for the defendant, the lawyer must review her own client's documents. This enables the lawyer to effectively strategize for the long term and to draft a pleading consistent with this long-term strategy. If the lawyer sees her own client's documents only after the pleading, or initial exchange of documents, changes may need to be made to both the strategy and the pleading. This increases legal fees. I urge all clients to give their lawyers all their documents as early in the proceedings as possible. A lawyer who understands the strengths and weaknesses of her client's case early in the proceeding can attempt to settle the matter. At the very least, while still early in the process, she can instruct her client about the challenges ahead.

As well, there may be documents, seemingly unimportant to the advisor, which the lawyer considers helpful to the advisor's case. A note in the advisor's diary, for instance, could be proof of a meeting that the client denies took place. A good lawyer may be able to use the documents to discourage the plaintiff's counsel from pursuing the case. For instance, the lawyer may point out gaping holes in the plaintiff's case. Early in the process, this could lead to no or nominal payment for the plaintiff in exchange for an early dismissal of the claim.

Once the advisor's lawyer receives the opponent's documents, it may be appropriate for the advisor to ask the lawyer to assess the strengths and weaknesses of his defense against his former client, the plaintiff.

ORAL EXAMINATIONS/DEPOSITIONS

After the exchange of pleadings and documents, each party's lawyer has the opportunity to examine the opposite party. In some jurisdictions, you can examine only one person; in others, you can examine parties and witnesses. As long as the questions asked are relevant and not privileged, they must be answered.

What makes a question privileged? Entire legal texts are written on the subject of privilege, and the laws vary to some degree between jurisdictions. The basic rule is that communication between a lawyer and client is protected. The advisor's lawyer can explain the law on this issue and can instruct the advisor not to answer questions that relate to privileged communication.

SETTLEMENT MEETING/PRE-TRIAL

Before trial there is usually a settlement meeting, sometimes with a judge who will not hear the case at trial. The judge reviews the pertinent documents and encourages the parties to settle the case. It is up to the parties and their respective lawyers to determine whether a meeting is appropriate to attempt to settle the case. Such a meeting may be just between lawyers, or it may include clients, and/or, possibly, a third-party facilitator.[2] Sometimes the lawyers do not feel they have sufficient information to settle the case. They may, therefore, insist on examining the other party before attempting to settle the case. Other cases may be sufficiently ripe for settlement, based only on an exchange of documents. In my view, lawyers should not wait until this stage of the proceeding to raise the possibility of settling. Instead, they should discuss this option with their clients throughout the process. Litigation is very costly. The earlier in the proceeding the lawyer can settle the case, the lower the client's legal fees will be.

If the matter cannot be settled at this stage, then the lawyers will prepare for trial. Witnesses will be prepared, including expert witnesses, who are necessary in most cases between a client and an advisor. Expert witnesses are most commonly used in this type of case to provide opinions on calculations of damages, suitability, and industry practice.

TRIAL

A trial can last anywhere from a day to several months. Most cases against advisors proceed for at least several days. Each party calls witnesses to testify, and the opposing party has an opportunity to cross-examine. The plaintiff (the client) suing usually takes the witness stand first. After each of the plaintiff's witnesses testify, the advisor's lawyer cross-examines them, attempting to discredit their testimony.

---

2. This is referred to as mediation, but this topic is beyond the scope of this book.

After the plaintiff's witnesses have all been called to the witness box and have been examined and cross-examined, it is the defendant's turn to call witnesses.

Usually, the defendant's lawyer calls witnesses, whom she examines. After each examination of a witness by the defendant's lawyer, the plaintiff's lawyer cross-examines that same witness.

After all the witnesses have testified, closing arguments are made by each of the lawyers. This is the dramatic part usually seen in movies and on television. The lawyers try to convince the judge or jury to rule in their respective client's favor.

As I've mentioned before in this book, most advisors find that judges view them much less sympathetically than they view the advisor's former client, the plaintiff. In contrast, the advisor is depicted by the plaintiff, the plaintiff's lawyer, and the media as a "rogue broker." When the suing client is older, uneducated, and unsophisticated, the advisor should expect the judge to be biased in the plaintiff's favor. That is why it is crucial for advisors to have documentation supporting their version of events. If advisors rely on oral testimony alone, clients will have a huge advantage in the case.

Most clients do not take notes during their meetings or telephone conversations with their advisors. Therefore, only one version of notes describing meetings and telephone calls likely exists. If the notes corroborate the advisor's version of events, then the advisor may prove that the poor, unsophisticated, uneducated client is lying; while, the sophisticated, professional advisor is telling the truth. Proper documentation tells the story better than anything else.

There are several insurance cases in which the plaintiff, or the insured, suffers a loss, and the insurance company denies coverage. The plaintiff sues the agent, the broker, the insurance company, and any other individual or entity that was part of the transaction. In cases where there are no notes, e-mails, or letters to the client confirming exclusions in coverage, judges have not hesitated to order that the "deep-pocket" broker, agent, or insurance company compensate the plaintiff/client.

ADVISORS TAKE ACTION

✓ Understand that settling with a client in legal proceedings may be appropriate in certain circumstances. It may also have the benefit of being confidential.

✓ Realize that the release signed by the client cannot and will not prohibit the client from issuing a complaint to the regulator.

✓ Work with your lawyer to prepare accurate pleadings.

✓ Provide all documentation to your lawyer, even documents that are detrimental to your case.

✓ Appreciate how notes and documents can corroborate your testimony.

CHAPTER 12
Regulatory Investigations—Summary

How does an advisor get caught in the web of a regulatory investigation?

There are several ways in which an advisor can become the target of an investigation. The most common, but certainly not the only, way is when a client complains to the regulator about the advisor's activities.

A. **Regulatory Surprise Audit**—In most jurisdictions, the regulator does not need the advisor's or dealer's permission to audit the dealer, branch, or an individual advisor's files. In fact, the regulator can and does perform surprise audits in which the dealer has no opportunity to organize the office files before the regulator appears. During such an audit, the regulator is entitled to inspect any and all files and obtain copies of all materials. Such materials can be taken back to the regulator's offices to ponder, while the regulator considers whether a further investigation is necessary or appropriate.

B. **Regulatory Scheduled Audit**—The regulator can schedule an audit with the dealer. You can well imagine the flurry of activity to clean up the office between the time notice is given and the time the regulator arrives. While a tidy office may provide investigators with a positive first impression, it will not deter them from delving into the files to ensure they contain up-to-date KYCs and proper documentation. Accounts may be examined for suitability, and branch manager's files may be reviewed to determine if advisors are being properly supervised. Such an audit may result in a letter listing infractions and providing a deadline by which certain steps must be taken. However, in most jurisdictions, it is within the regulator's authority to begin a more detailed investigation or to begin proceedings as a result of audit findings.

C. **The dealer notifies the regulator**—In certain jurisdictions, there is a regulatory obligation to report complaints, lawsuits, settlements, and certain very limited, extreme infractions. Dealers are free to handle infractions that do not fall into one of the above three categories. They may handle violations through internal discipline or dismissal. Both internal discipline and dismissal can take place without the dealer reporting to the regulator. In the limited circumstance of dismissal for cause, however, the infraction must be reported on the Uniform Termination Notice.

PROCESS AND PROCEDURE

What is it about an advisor receiving a letter from his regulator that makes him sweat? Is it fear that the regulator has received a client complaint? Is it the threat of a large penalty? Does the advisor fear losing his license? Is he wary of bad publicity in the local media? Most likely, it is all of the above.

To help dispel the anxiety associated with a regulatory investigation, I will describe the stages of the proceeding and what advisors should expect at each stage:

INITIAL CONTACT

A regulatory inquiry almost always begins with a letter. Sometimes, however, someone from the regulator's office simply calls the advisor at work and directs him to come to the regulator's office for an interview. The advisor breaks into a sweat, wishing that he could change history.

The advisor, wanting the matter to disappear, chooses to keep it a secret, failing to notify his dealer, his branch manager, or even a lawyer, who could prepare him for the interview and represent him through the process. This is a big mistake. First of all, the advisor's dealer is experienced in such matters and can assist the advisor through the process. Most jurisdictions and the internal policies of dealers require advisors to notify their dealers when the regulator begins an investigation. The dealer and branch manager may also be under investigation for activities associated with allegations against the advisor. Therefore, the dealer and branch manager or supervisor must be notified.

Secondly, the dealer has resources, including in-house or external lawyers, who can prepare the advisor for the interview and go with him. Such preparation allows advisors to anticipate the questions they will eventually be asked and to prepare proper (always honest) answers. While the lawyer will emphasize the advisor's obligation to tell the truth at the interview, the advisor will be far more confident having been prepared. There are several ways to answer a question truthfully. Preparation means the difference between the advisor putting his best or worst foot forward. It is normal to be very nervous before the interview. Without preparation, the advisor may answer in ways that do more harm than good. The advisor will feel more confident if he is prepared with answers to questions, ahead of time. In part, the regulatory investigators will judge the advisor's honesty. If the advisor is not prepared, he may not be as confident with his answers and may appear dishonest.

Finally, a lawyer experienced in this area is an ally at the interview. Advisors may be more comfortable at the interview in the presence of a supportive and knowledgeable lawyer, especially since the regulator usually has more than one person conducting the interview. For the advisor's own sake, it is best not to keep secret an interview with the regulator.

As soon as the advisor receives a letter from the regulator, he should tell his branch manager. The branch manager then determines who should be notified in the compliance and/or legal departments. The advisor may be directed to prepare an internal memo that provides the dealer with background information. The advisor will want such a memo to remain confidential, especially if the client is pursuing litigation against the advisor in regard to the same issues arising in the regulatory investigation. The advisor should ask questions to confirm that his dealer has taken the necessary steps to ensure that the memo does not have to be divulged to the lawyer of the advisor's former client. The issue of protecting the document, however, is beyond the scope of this book.

DOCUMENTATION REQUESTS

The investigator may request documentation. The KYC form interests the investigator when the complaint involves suitability. The advisor, aided by a compliance officer or lawyer, should comply with the request and prepare a package. The regulator's investigator will analyze the documentation and decide whether to recommend to senior regulatory officials that the file be closed or further pursued.

Annoying the investigator is not advisable. At this stage, co-operation is the name of the game. What happens if an advisor does not co-operate with the regulator? That depends on the particular jurisdiction involved. An advisor should seek advice from a local lawyer on this subject.

THE INTERVIEW

If the case is pursued, an interview or examination by the regulatory staff is scheduled. The advisor should meet with his lawyer before the interview to prepare for possible questions. By this stage, the advisor's lawyer should be able to anticipate the issues of concern and the questions that will be asked.

Being prepared by an experienced lawyer, who may or may not be part of the dealer's in-house team, is crucial because the tape and documentation of the interview is the foundation for the regulator's case against the advisor.

WAITING AND WAITING AND WAITING

After the interview, there may be a long delay before the regulator acts. Although regulators in most jurisdictions have limitation periods to which they must adhere, months, and even years, can pass without a single word from the regulator. I have been involved in matters that have spanned long periods. Recently, however, regulators have had strict timelines. They worry that the matter may be dismissed if they fail to prosecute in a timely manner, especially if they do not prosecute before the limitation period expires.

Advisors report that the waiting period is the worst part of the process. While waiting, the advisor prays and wishes that the matter would simply vanish, but he knows that is not going to happen, and usually, it doesn't. At the advisor's request, his lawyer can try to move the matter along. Eventually, the regulator will determine if the file will be closed or if it intends to refer the matter to enforcement for a hearing.

SETTLEMENT NEGOTIATIONS

Settlement negotiations usually occur before the hearing. The advisor and his lawyer will discuss the relative strengths and weaknesses of the regulator's case. If the regulator's evidence is strong, the advisor may choose to settle. Many advisors choose to settle because the outcome of a hearing is uncertain, and they want to finish with it. The settlement offer may include any one of or a combination of the following penalties: a financial penalty; a separate sum to reimburse the regulator for the costs of investigating the matter; a requirement that the advisor take certain courses; and/or a revocation of, or restriction to, the advisor's license. In most jurisdictions, the regulatory tribunal must approve the settlement terms for the settlement to be final.

If the matter cannot be settled, a hearing is scheduled. At the hearing, the investigator testifies; afterwards, the advisor's lawyer cross-examines the investigator. To prove the regulatory infractions, the regulator's lawyer may rely on the transcript or tape of the interview with the advisor. After the regulator's lawyer has called all her witnesses, including, perhaps, the complaining client, the advisor's lawyer calls her witnesses. The advisor, and in certain circumstances his witnesses, each attempt to rebut the regulator's testimony with their own evidence, upon which they are cross-examined. Other witnesses can be called; for example, each party can call expert witnesses.

After all evidence is provided, the lawyers conclude with statements; and the regulatory tribunal, usually a panel of three, makes a decision and provides reasons for the decision. The panel decides whether there was a violation, the amount of the penalty, and whether or not the advisor's license will be suspended or revoked. In most jurisdictions, the decision and the penalty can be appealed within a court of law. However, this prolongs the resolution and is expensive because legal costs associated with such an appeal can be substantial.

ADVISORS TAKE ACTION

✓ Understand that regulators may commence an investigation with or without a client complaint.

✓ Realize that an investigation and enforcement proceedings can take several months or years.

✓ Use your dealer's resources. Staff in both compliance and legal departments can help you.

✓ Seek a lawyer's help when preparing for a regulatory interview. The lawyer can also accompany you to the interview.

✓ Obtain advice about the importance of co-operating with the regulator in your jurisdiction.

CONCLUSION

Writing this book has been a labor of love. It has taken me more than two years of weekends and holidays to write. My sincere hope is that this book provides advisors and dealers with a better understanding of their roles and responsibilities as professionals, and with an appreciation of industry risks and their underlying causes. With this book, advisors have a roadmap to reduce their risks and protect their businesses.

This book was written to help advisors better understand their obligations, including the responsibility to know their clients in much greater depth than is possible through the KYC form. With an enhanced understanding of their clients, advisors can better:

- prove the conclusions summarized in the KYC form;
- ensure that all investments are suitable;
- understand the importance of explaining the risk of each product; and
- appreciate the importance of documenting all aspects of their relationships with their clients.

Doing all of the above contributes to an advisor's credibility in court and at the regulator. This means an advisor's version of events is more likely to be believed.

The examples given, as well as the checklists and headings, were designed to make the book easy to navigate. They were also designed to give advisors a renewed appreciation for their supervisors and compliance officers. These people can save an advisor's most valuable assets: his or her reputation, license, and, of course, livelihood.

Good luck and all the best to you.

— Ellen

ELLEN BESSNER

Ms. Bessner was a litigation partner at a national law firm and, since January 2014, has been practising law at Babin Bessner Spry LLP.. She regularly represents financial institutions, brokerage firms, corporations and individuals in all aspects of commercial and securities issues, employment law, and professional liability, including investment advisors, registered representatives, financial advisors, branch managers, CEOs, CFOs, COOs, CCOs, compliance officers, insurance brokers, insurance agents, and MGAs.

Ms. Bessner appears before the Superior Court of Ontario and the Ontario Court of Appeal, and various tribunals, including the IIROC, MFDA, OSC and FSCO. Ms. Bessner is a regular speaker at industry (MFDA, IIROC, Provincial Securities Commissions, IFIC, Advocis, ACCP) and dealer conferences. She writes regularly for the National Post and has written extensively for industry publications on matters of risk management and compliance, has co-written a paper on investment advisor's liability for the Canadian Securities Institute's continuing education program, and published a paper on the Fair Dealing Model.

Ms. Bessner offers compliance, risk management and AML courses to dealers, for Compliance Officers, Branch Managers, Advisors and Institutional Traders, which have been recognized by SROs and industry organizations for Continuing Education credits. See:

www.babinbessnerspry.com

Ms. Bessner has been retained by MFDA members, and recognized by the MFDA as an Independent Consultant for testing and reporting purposes. Ms. Bessner was called to the Ontario Bar in 1989 after completing her LLB at Osgoode Hall Law School and her Bachelor of Commerce at McGill University.

Index

175

179

Made in the USA
Monee, IL
08 June 2021